Arbeitsblätter für den
berufsbezogenen Englischunterricht

Technisches Englisch 1

Hubertus Bleich

westermann

1. Key to the work sheets

Lesson

2. Vokabeltests

Page

Lesson

3. Klassenarbeiten

Page

Lesson

4. Kopiervorlagen für OH-Folien

Page

Lesson

5. Quiz – questions on book 1

Page

Introducing people 1

Lesson **1.0**

Here are the people who work in a small company in Bristol:

1. Jason is an electrician.
2. He is 1.80 m tall.
3. He is 40 years old and single.
4. He likes hamburgers, discos, going out, flirting, and rugby.
5. He hates rap music but loves funky stuff.

1. Ahmed is a mechanic.
2. He is 1.87 metres tall.
3. He is 25 years old and married. He has a son and two daughters.
4. He likes kebabs, big cars, karate, and soccer.
5. He loves pop songs and hates heavy metal.

1. Rick is a trainee.
2. He is 1.75 metres tall.
3. He is 17 years old and has a nice girl-friend.
4. He likes coke, hamburgers, motorbikes, American football, wrestling, and beer.
5. He dislikes pop but enjoys punk and house music.

1. Duncan is the boss.
2. He is very tall.
3. He is 58 years old, married and has three children.
4. He likes hard work and has no time for sports. His job is his life.
5. He sometimes listens to classical music.

What's your job? How tall are you? How old are you? What do you like?

I am a student.
I am 1.85 m tall.
I am 18 and have two girl-friends.
I like pizza and rap music best.

I am an engineer.
I am 1.72 m tall.
I am 32 and married.
I like soccer and the cooking of my wife.

Introducing people 2

Lesson **1.0**

Basic verbs:

to eat, to drink, to sleep

to love, to like, to hate, to enjoy

to listen, to watch, to see, to hear

to go, to work, to kiss, to forget, to read

to smell, to feel, to taste

to speak, to explain

to have, to be

I	*am*	*I*	*like*
you	*are*	*you*	*like*
he	*is*	*he*	*likes*
she	*is*	*she*	*likes*
it	*is*	*it*	*likes*
we	*are*	*we*	*like*
you	*are*	*you*	*like*
they	*are*	*they*	*like*

Introduce your father the same way as overleaf.

1. *He is an engineer.*
2. *He is 1.85 m tall.*
3. *He is 45 and divorced.*
4. *He likes boxing.*
5. *He hates ice-cream.*

Introduce your girl-friend.

1. *She is a nurse.*
2. *She is 1.60 m tall.*
3. *She is 16.*
4. *She likes dancing.*
5. *She hates Italian food.*

Introduce your work group at your company.

1. *We are plumbers.*
2. *We are all very tall.*
3. *We are all about 40.*
4. *We like our work.*
5. *We hate Mondays.*

Introduce a famous person. Let the others guess the name afterwards.

1. *He is a pop star.*
2. *He is 1.73 m tall.*
3. *He is 34.*
4. *He likes children.*
5. *He hates dust and dirt.*

1. *What's your best friend's job?* — *He is a teacher.*
2. *How tall is the Eiffel Tower?* — *It is over 300 metres.*
3. *How old is the London Tower?* — *It is over 800 years old.*
4. *What sports do you like?* — *I like badminton.*
5. *What is your favourite meal?* — *My favourite meal is pizza.*
6. *How many hours do you work?* — *I normally work 8 hours.*

Tools – and how to work with them   Lesson **1.1**

1. You can smooth things with a file.
2. You can hold things with a pair of pliers.
3. You can undo bolts with a spanner.
4. You can cut wood with a saw.
5. You can tighten screws with a screwdriver.
6. You can drill holes with a drill.

What can you do with these tools?
Make sentences!

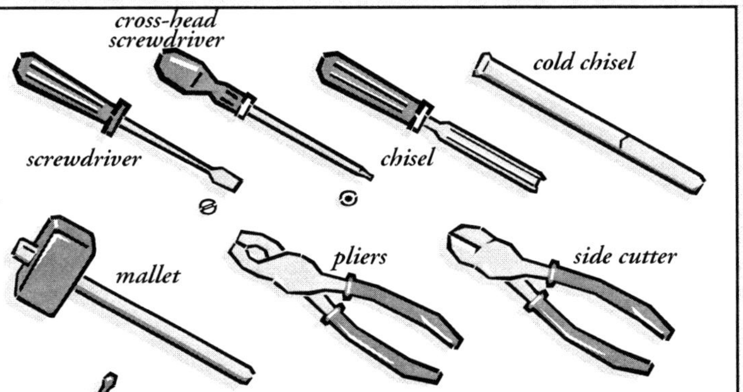

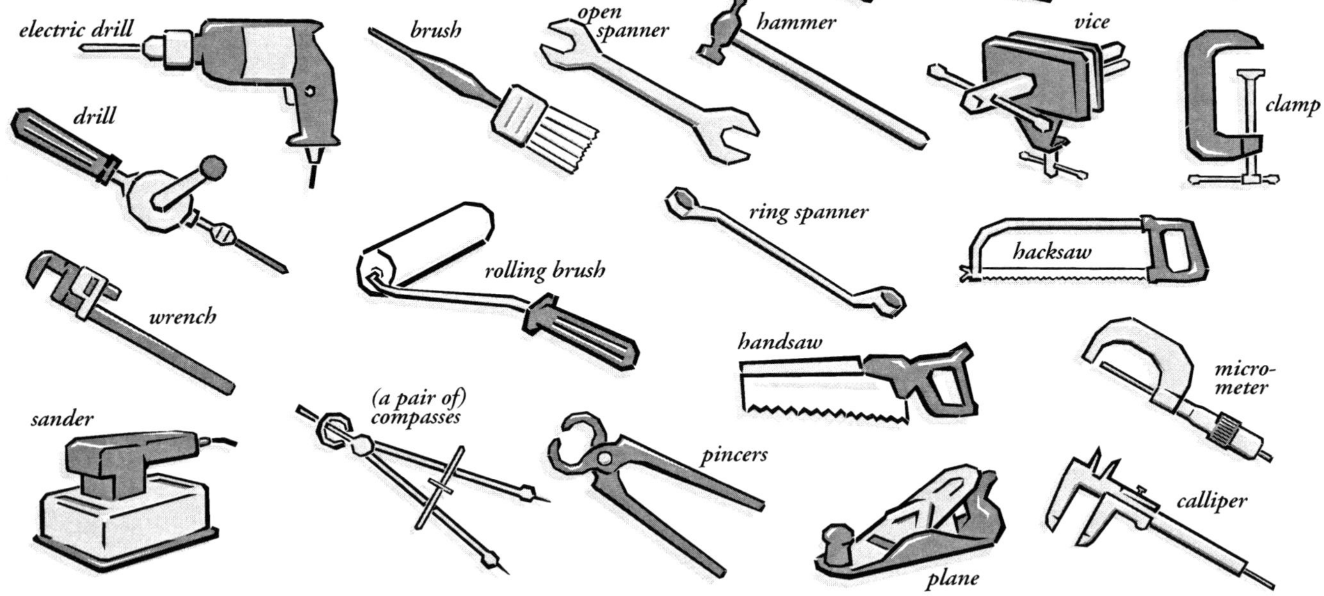

	put in			a drill.
	cut	screws		a file.
	bend	nails		a spanner.
You (can)	smooth	nuts and bolts	in	a pair of pliers.
	drill	small things	with	a saw.
	do up/undo	holes		a hammer.
	hit	things		a vice.
	hold			a screwdriver.

You can put in screws with a screwdriver.

You can cut things with a saw.

You can bend small things in a vice.

You can smooth things with a file.

You can drill holes with a drill.

You can undo nuts with a spanner.

You can hit nails with a hammer.

You can hold things in a vice.

1. You can smooth things with a file.
2. You can hold things with a pair of pliers.
3. You can undo bolts with a spanner.
4. You can cut wood with a saw.
5. You can tighten screws with a screwdriver.
6. You can drill holes with a drill.

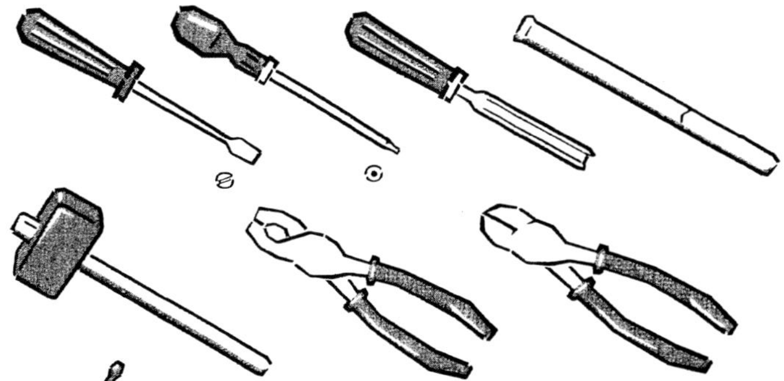

What can you do with these tools?
Make sentences!

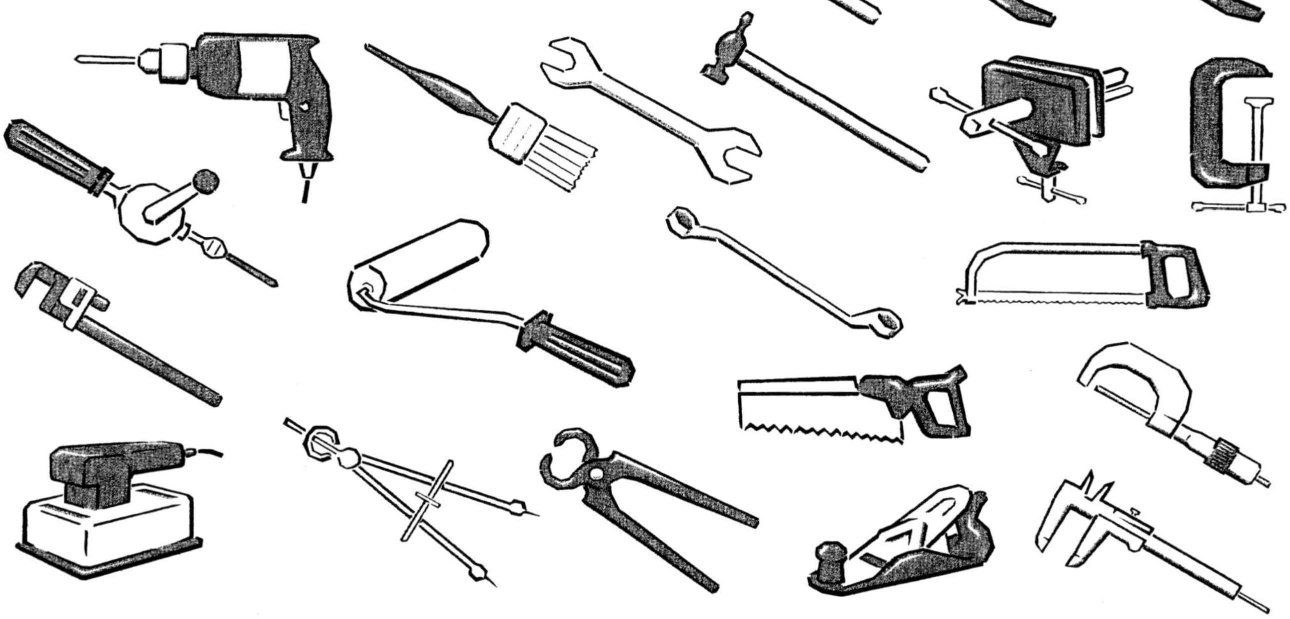

	put in			a drill.
	cut	screws		a file.
	bend	nails		a spanner.
You (can)	smooth	nuts and bolds	in	a pair of pliers.
	drill	small things	with	a saw.
	do up/undo	holes		a hammer.
	hit	things		a vice.
	hold			a screwdriver.

Tools – and how to work with them

Lesson **1.1**

Complete this list.

	Tools	Profession	Verbs

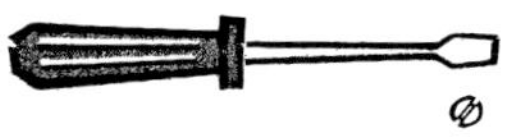			
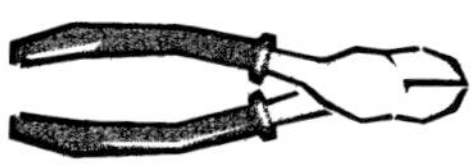			
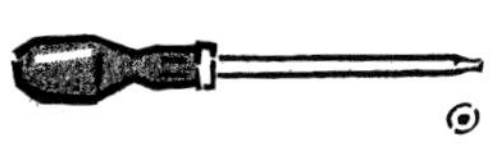			
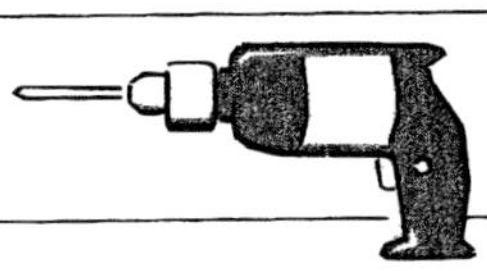			

1. Use the information given to produce questions and small sentences like these:

1. Who uses a file? — A mechanic uses a file to smooth rough objects.
2. What can you do with a hammer? — With a hammer you can drive nails in.
3. Which tools does a joiner use? — A joiner uses a mallet for woodwork.
4. What is a clamp used for? — A clamp is used for holding things.

2. Now ask people in the classroom the same way.

Tools – and how to work with them

Lesson **1.1**

1. You can smooth things with a file.
2. You can hold things with a pair of pliers.
3. You can undo bolts with a spanner.
4. You can cut wood with a saw.
5. You can tighten screws with a screwdriver.
6. You can drill holes with a drill.

What can you do with these tools?
Make sentences!

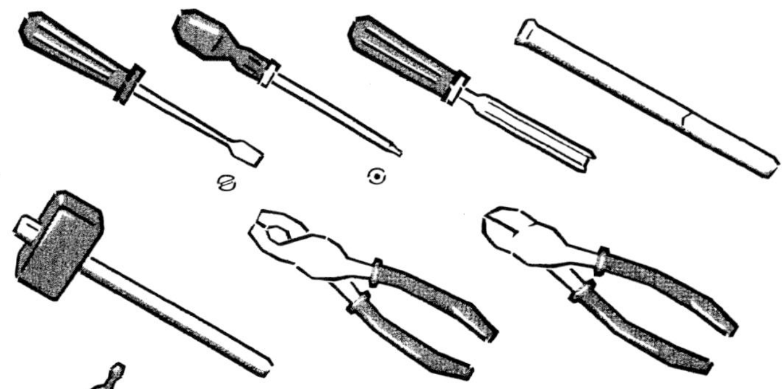

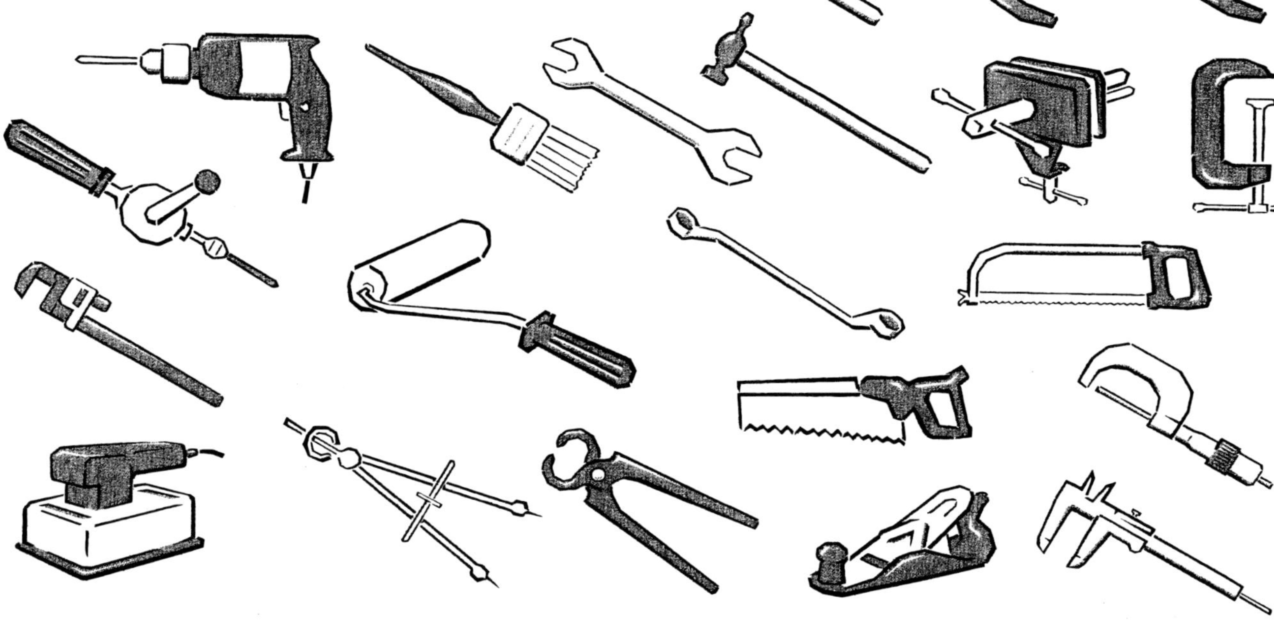

	put in			a drill.
	cut	screws		a file.
	bend	nails		a spanner.
You (can)	smooth	nuts and bolds	in	a pair of pliers.
	drill	small things	with	a saw.
	do up/undo	holes		a hammer.
	hit	things		a vice.
	hold			a screwdriver.

Tools – and how to work with them

Complete this list.

	Tools	Profession	Verbs

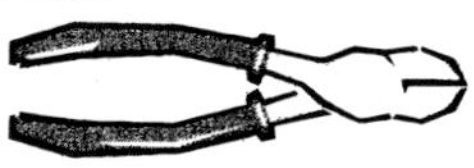			
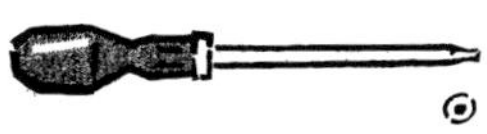			
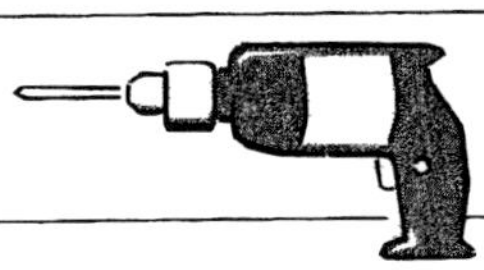			

1. Use the information given to produce questions and small sentences like these:

1. Who uses a file? — A mechanic uses a file to smooth rough objects.
2. What can you do with a hammer? — With a hammer you can drive nails in.
3. Which tools does a joiner use? — A joiner uses a mallet for woodwork.
4. What is a clamp used for? — A clamp is used for holding things.

....

....

....

....

....

....

....

2. Now ask people in the classroom the same way.

1. You can smooth things with a file.
2. You can hold things with a pair of pliers.
3. You can undo bolts with a spanner.
4. You can cut wood with a saw.
5. You can tighten screws with a screwdriver.
6. You can drill holes with a drill.

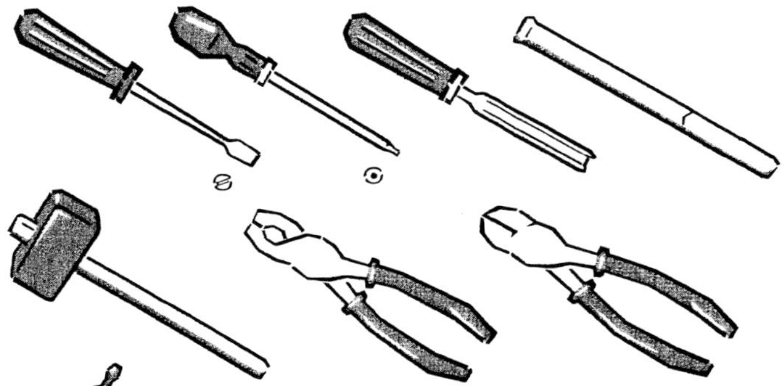

What can you do with these tools?
Make sentences!

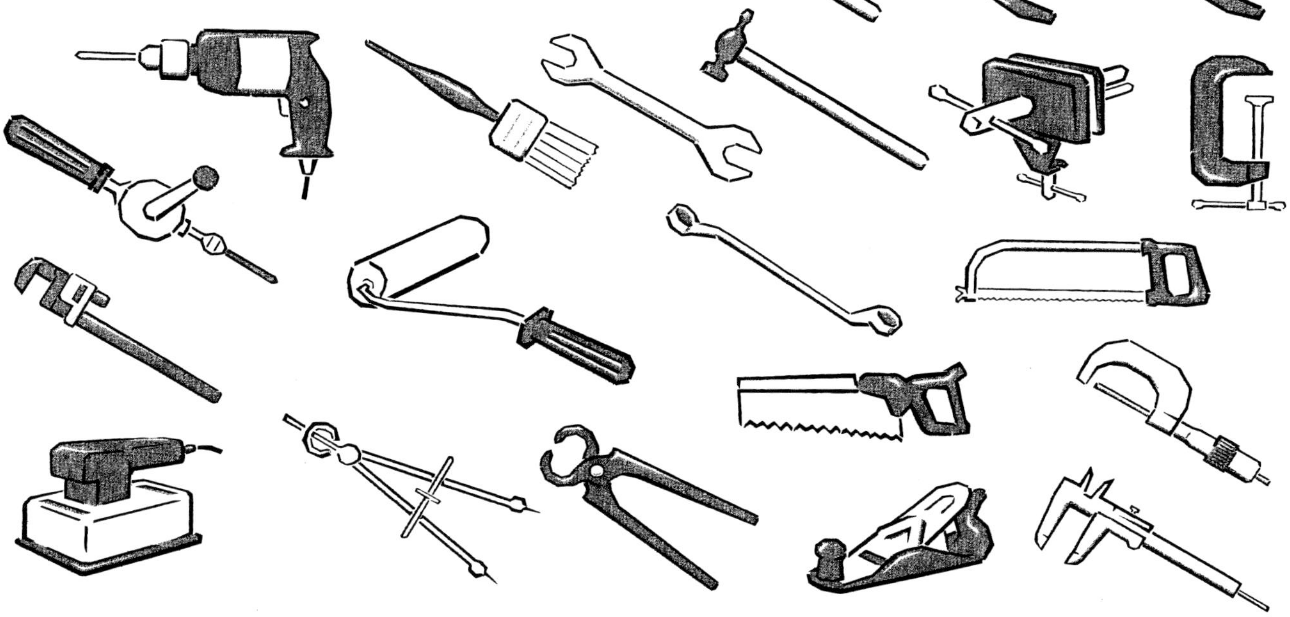

	put in			a drill.
	cut	screws		a file.
	bend	nails		a spanner.
You (can)	smooth	nuts and bolds	in	a pair of pliers.
	drill	small things	with	a saw.
	do up/undo	holes		a hammer.
	hit	things		a vice.
	hold			a screwdriver.

Tools – and how to work with them

Complete this list.

	Tools	Profession	Verbs

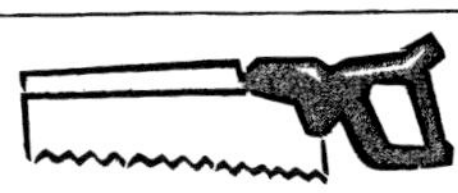			

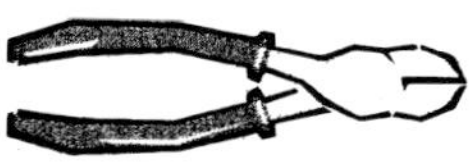			

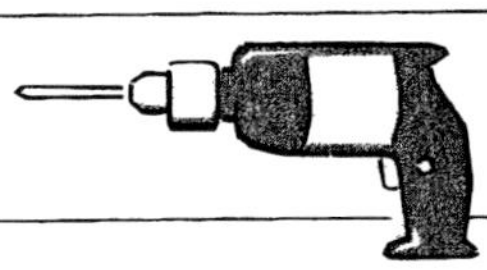			

1. *Use the information given to produce questions and small sentences like these:*

1. Who uses a file?	A mechanic uses a file to smooth rough objects.
2. What can you do with a hammer?	With a hammer you can drive nails in.
3. Which tools does a joiner use?	A joiner uses a mallet for woodwork.
4. What is a clamp used for?	A clamp is used for holding things.

2. *Now ask people in the classroom the same way.*

1. You can smooth things with a file.
2. You can hold things with a pair of pliers.
3. You can undo bolts with a spanner.
4. You can cut wood with a saw.
5. You can tighten screws with a screwdriver.
6. You can drill holes with a drill.

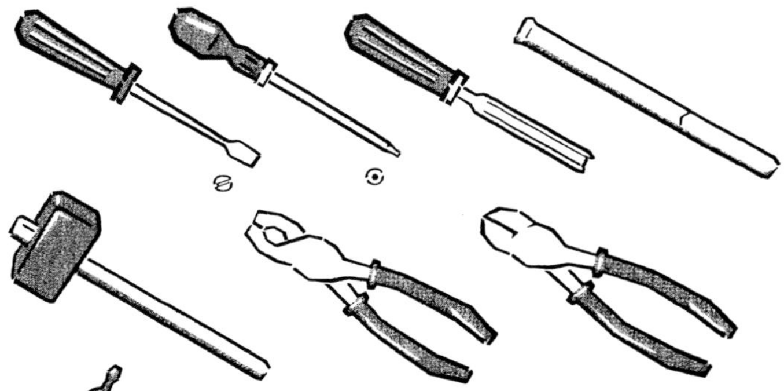

What can you do with these tools?
Make sentences!

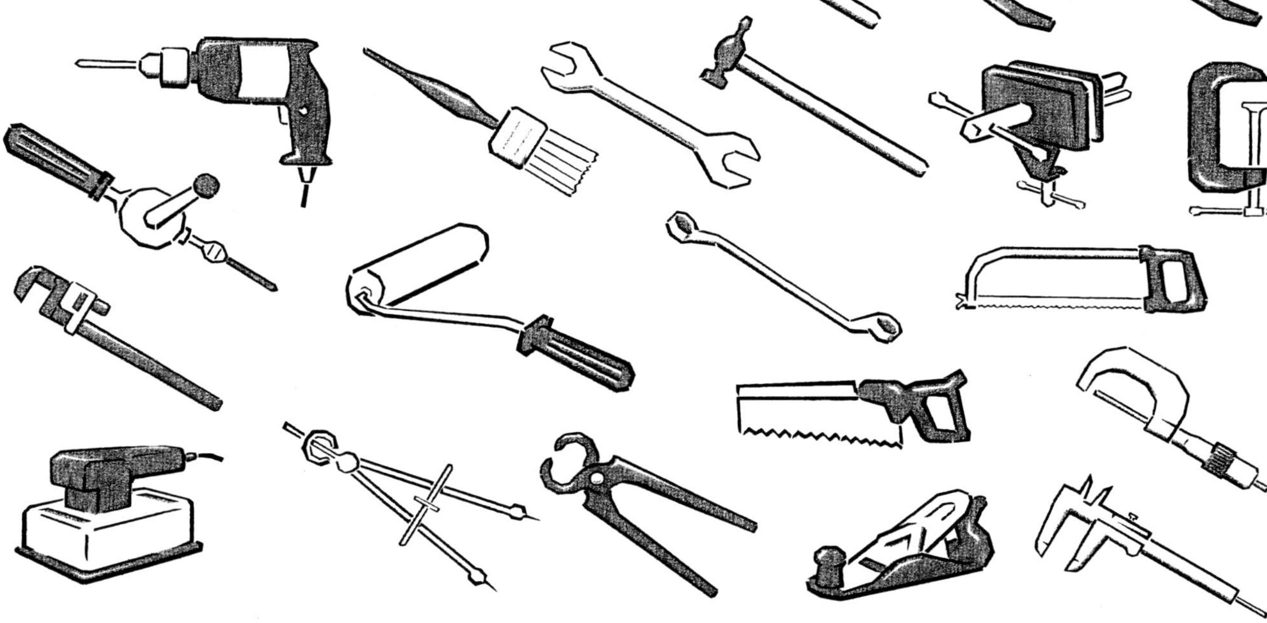

You (can)	put in cut bend smooth drill do up/undo hit hold	screws nails nuts and bolds small things holes things	in with	a drill. a file. a spanner. a pair of pliers. a saw. a hammer. a vice. a screwdriver.

Tools – and how to work with them

Lesson **1.1**

Complete this list.

	Tools	Profession	Verbs

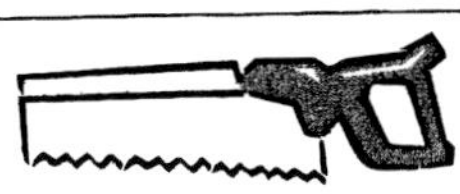			
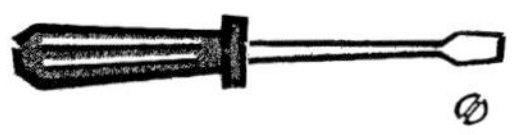			
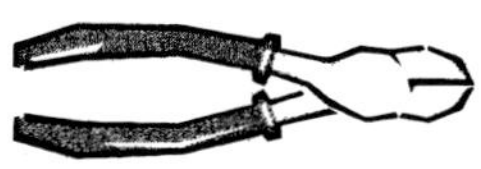			

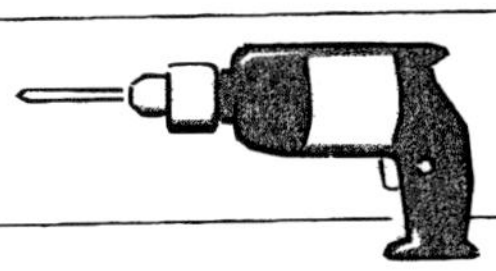			

1. Use the information given to produce questions and small sentences like these:

1. Who uses a file? — A mechanic uses a file to smooth rough objects.
2. What can you do with a hammer? — With a hammer you can drive nails in.
3. Which tools does a joiner use? — A joiner uses a mallet for woodwork.
4. What is a clamp used for? — A clamp is used for holding things.

....

....

....

....

....

....

....

2. Now ask people in the classroom the same way.

1. You can smooth things with a file.
2. You can hold things with a pair of pliers.
3. You can undo bolts with a spanner.
4. You can cut wood with a saw.
5. You can tighten screws with a screwdriver.
6. You can drill holes with a drill.

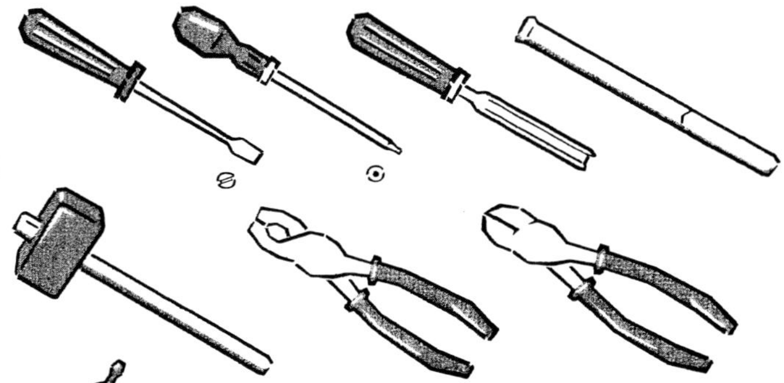

What can you do with these tools?
Make sentences!

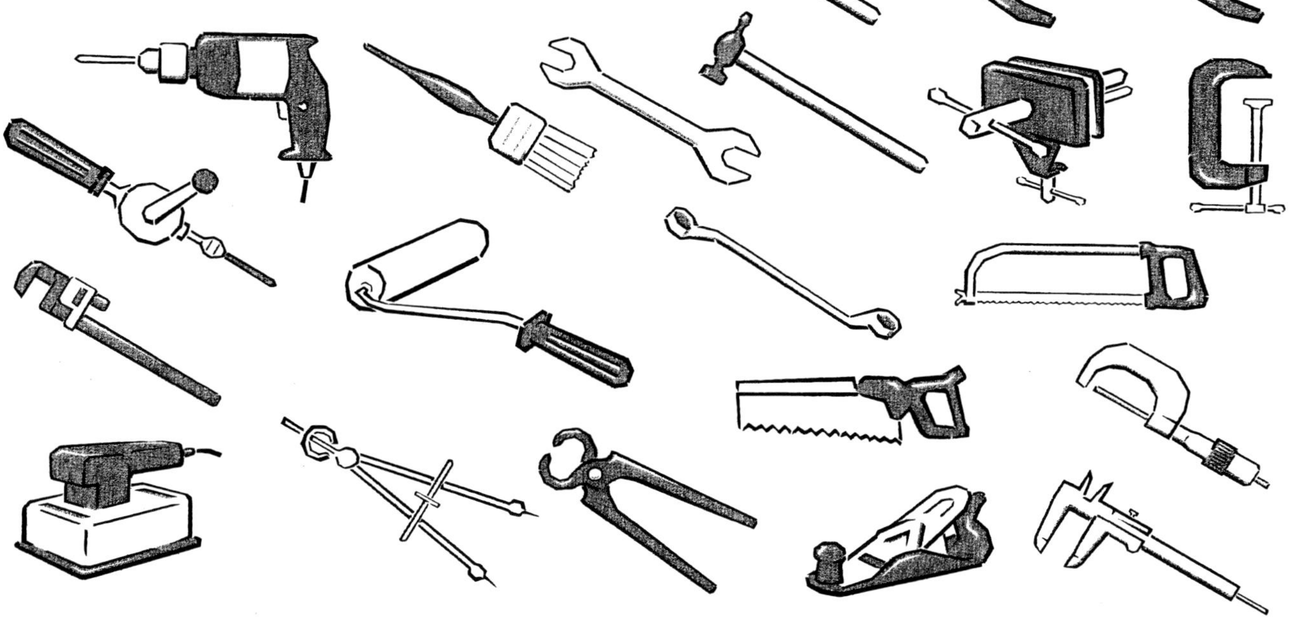

	put in			a drill.
	cut	screws		a file.
	bend	nails		a spanner.
You (can)	smooth	nuts and bolds	in	a pair of pliers.
	drill	small things	with	a saw.
	do up/undo	holes		a hammer.
	hit	things		a vice.
	hold			a screwdriver.

Tools – and how to work with them

Lesson **1.1**

Complete this list.

	Tools	**Profession**	**Verbs**

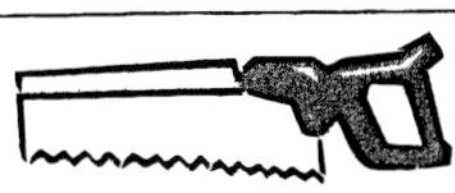			
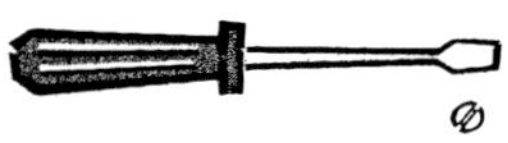			
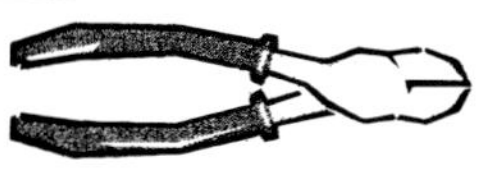			

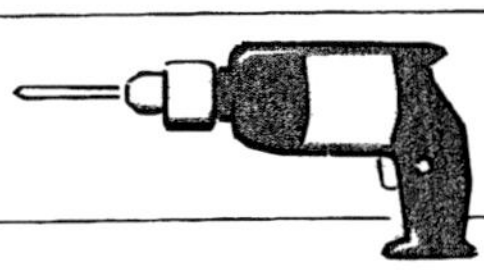			

1. *Use the information given to produce questions and small sentences like these:*

   1. Who uses a file? — A mechanic uses a file to smooth rough objects.
   2. What can you do with a hammer? — With a hammer you can drive nails in.
   3. Which tools does a joiner use? — A joiner uses a mallet for woodwork.
   4. What is a clamp used for? — A clamp is used for holding things.

2. *Now ask people in the classroom the same way.*

Tools – and how to work with them Lesson 1.1

1. You can smooth things with a file.
2. You can hold things with a pair of pliers.
3. You can undo bolts with a spanner.
4. You can cut wood with a saw.
5. You can tighten screws with a screwdriver.
6. You can drill holes with a drill.

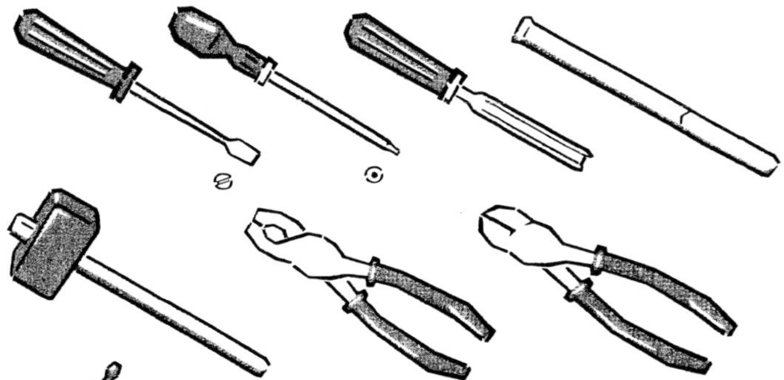

What can you do with these tools?
Make sentences!

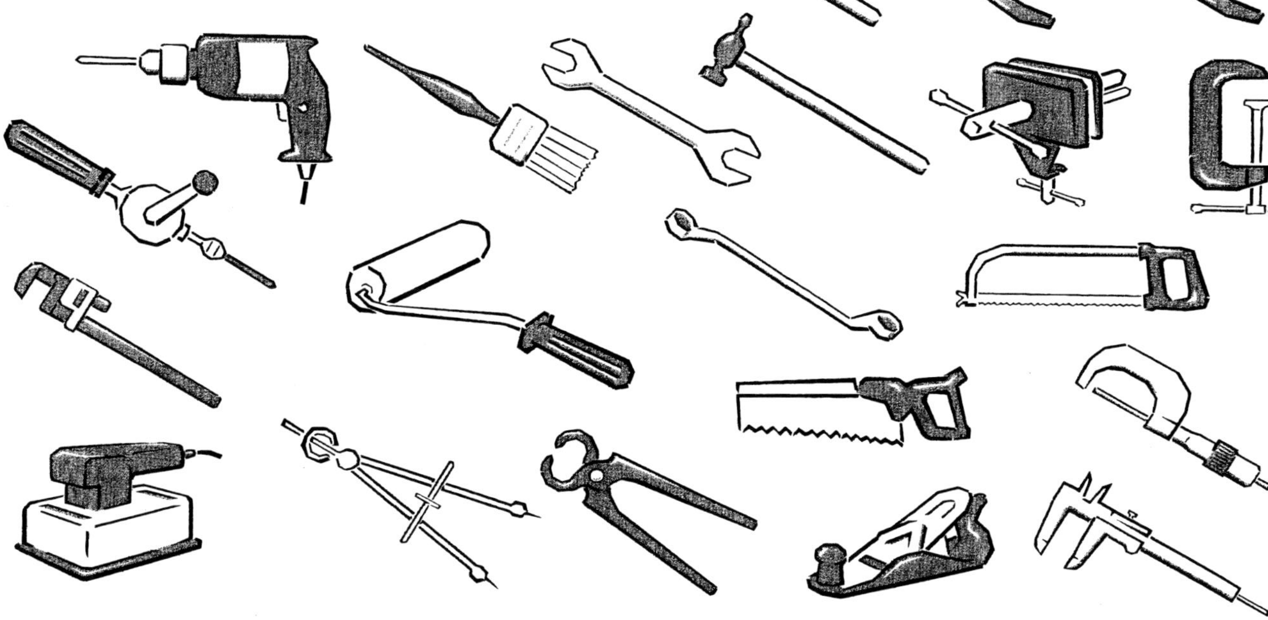

	put in			a drill.
	cut	screws		a file.
	bend	nails		a spanner.
You (can)	smooth	nuts and bolds	in	a pair of pliers.
	drill	small things	with	a saw.
	do up/undo	holes		a hammer.
	hit	things		a vice.
	hold			a screwdriver.

Tools – and how to work with them

Lesson **1.1**

Complete this list.

	Tools	Profession	Verbs

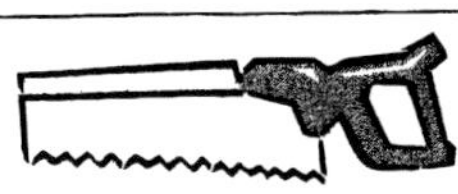			

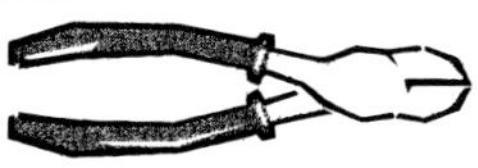			

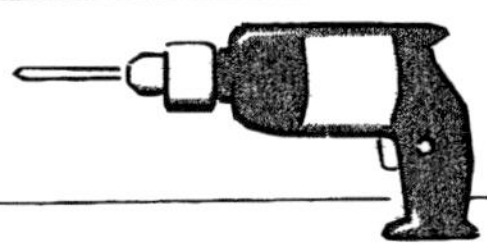			

1. Use the information given to produce questions and small sentences like these:

1. Who uses a file? — A mechanic uses a file to smooth rough objects.
2. What can you do with a hammer? — With a hammer you can drive nails in.
3. Which tools does a joiner use? — A joiner uses a mallet for woodwork.
4. What is a clamp used for? — A clamp is used for holding things.

....

....

....

....

....

....

....

2. Now ask people in the classroom the same way.

Complete this list.

	Tools	Profession	Verbs
	*file*	*mechanic*	*to smooth*
	*vice*	*metalworker*	*to hold*
	*hammer*	*plumber*	*to put in*
	*handsaw*	*carpenter*	*to saw*
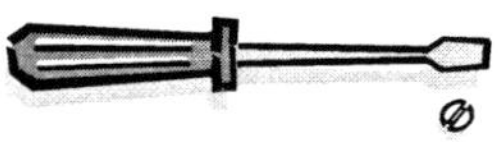	*screwdriver*	*electrician*	*to fix*
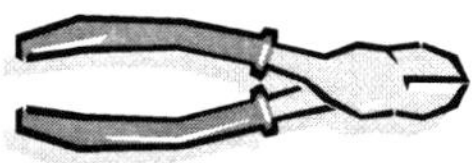	*side cutter*	*electrician*	*to cut*
	*cross-head screwdriver*	*mechanic*	*to undo*
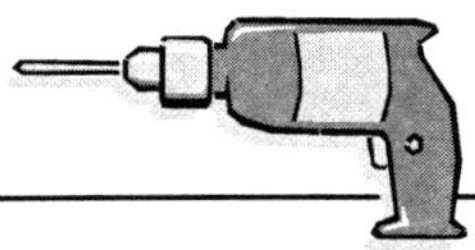	*electric drill*	*plumber*	*to drill*
	*chisel*	*mason bricklayer*	*to chisle*

1. *Use the information given to produce questions and small sentences like these:*
   1. Who uses a file? A mechanic uses a file to smooth rough objects.
   2. What can you do with a hammer? With a hammer you can drive nails in.
   3. Which tools does a joiner use? A joiner uses a mallet for woodwork.
   4. What is a clamp used for? A clamp is used for holding things.

5. Who uses a vice? A metalworker uses a vice to hold things.

6. Who uses a hammer? A plumber uses a hammer to put nails in.

7. What can you do with a handsaw?
With a handsaw you can saw wood.

8. Which tool does a mason use?
A mason uses a chisel to chisle holes into walls.

9. What is a side-cutter used for? It is used for cutting cables. etc.

2. *Now ask people in the classroom the same way.*

Tools and jobs 1

Lesson **1.2**

Form sentences this way:

A joiner cuts wood with a saw.
A plumber drills a hole into the pipe.

A painter paints *the wall with a brush.*

A tailor cuts *the cloth with a pair of scissors.*

An electrician bends *the cables.*

A car mechanic repairs *cars with a spanner.*

A technical draughtsman *makes plans.*

A carpenter *builds the roof of a house.*

With a file you can *smooth metal.*

With a pair of pliers you can *hold and cut things.*

With a hammer you can *drive in nails.*

to build (carpenter)

to wire (electrician)

to paint (painter)

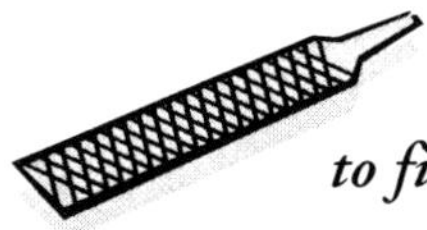

to file; to smooth

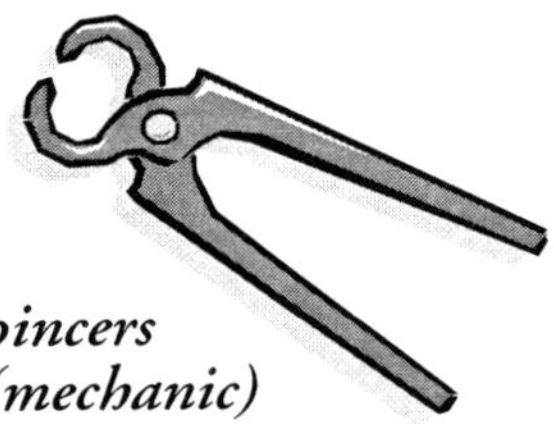

pincers (mechanic)

to nail (carpenter)

to saw (joiner)

1. The drivers *push* the brake.
2. When I come home I *switch on* the television.
3. If you want to open the door of the car, you must *pull* the handle.
4. If you like your girl-friend you *hold* her tight.
5. If the wood is too rough you *smooth* it.
6. When leaving the room you must *switch off* the light.
7. At the end of the party you must *empty* the ashtray.
8. Before working with an electric drill, you must *tighten* the chuck.
9. Before changing the wheel, you must *loosen* the nuts.
10. To open a can of coke, you *pull* the ring.

to switch on
to switch off
to press
to push
to pull
to hold
to tighten
to loosen
to plane
to fill
to empty

Tools and jobs 2

Lesson **1.2**

Here are some more tools.

Write under each drawing the name of the tool and the profession who uses it.

pair of pliers (mechanic)

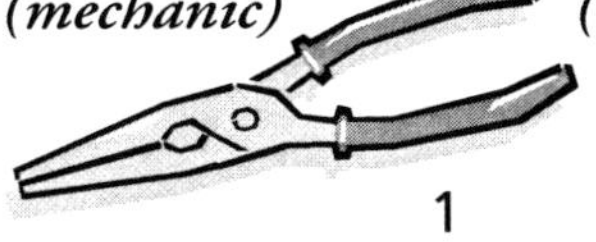

1

mole wrench (mechanic)

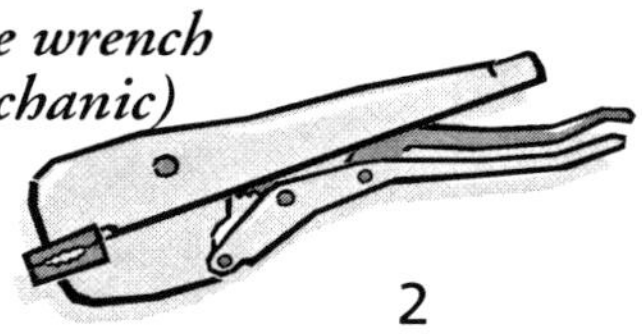

2

3

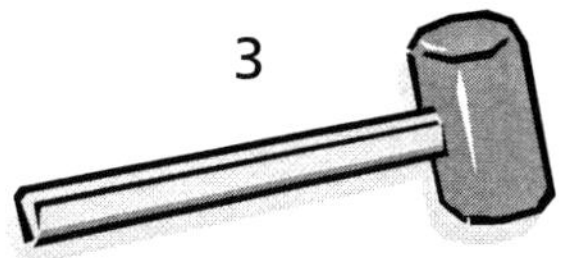

sledge hammer (mason)

scraper (mason, painter)

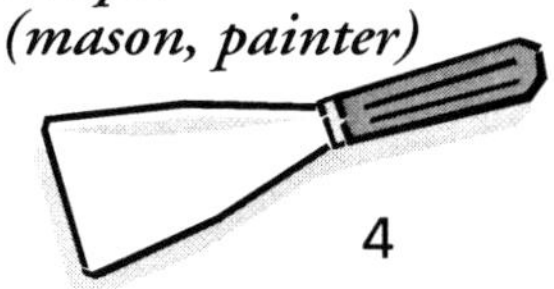

4

5

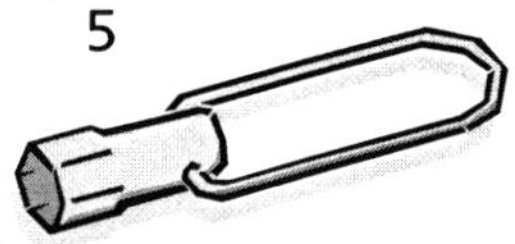

box spanner (car mechanic)

socket wrench

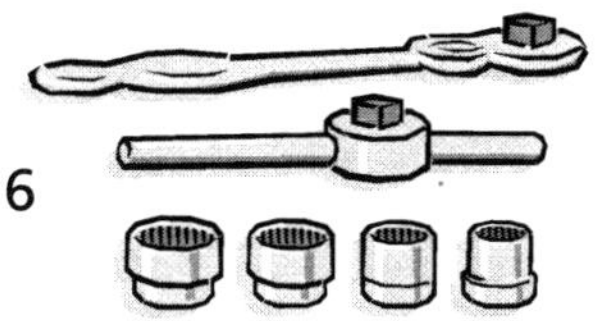

6

chisel (wood worker)

7

mains tester

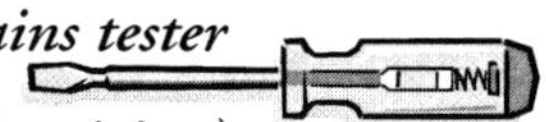

(electrician)

8

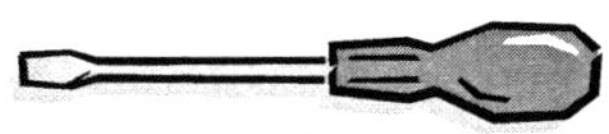

screwdriver (electrician)

9

10

hammer (bricklayer)

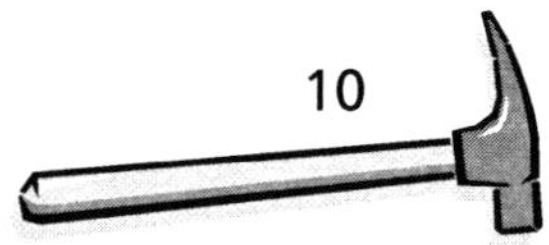

Form sentences like this:

1. A mechanic uses pincers for twisting wires.
2. *A mechanic uses a mole wrench for pressing things together.*
3. *A mason uses a sledge hammer for breaking stones.*
4. *A painter uses a scraper for removing wall paper.*
5. *A car mechanic uses a box spanner for undoing spark plugs.*
6. *A mechanic uses a socket wrench for tightening bolts.*
7. *An electrician uses a mains tester for testing currents.*
8. *A woodworker uses a chisel for cutting wood.*
9. *An electrician uses a screwdriver for loosening screws.*
10. *A bricklayer uses a hammer to cut stone.*

Write down the correct English term.		*Put in the profession who uses this tool.*
1. Steinmeißel	*cold chisel*	*mason, bricklayer*
2. Stechbeitel	*chisel*	*woodworker, painter*
3. Holzhammer	*mallet*	*carpenter, woodworker*
4. (Beiß-) Zange	*pincers*	*mechanic*
5. Grip-Zange	*mole wrench*	*mechanic, electrician*
6. Spannungsprüfer	*mains tester*	*electrician*
7. Schraubendreher	*screwdriver*	*nearly all professions*
8. Steckschlüssel	*box spanner (GB)* *socket wrench (USA)*	*mechanic*
9. Vierkantschlüssel	*spanner for square nuts*	*metalworker*
10. Maurerhammer	*sledge hammer*	*mason, bricklayer*
11. Universalschlüssel	*adjustable wrench*	*mechanic*

Option
Tools and jobs – working with an electric drill

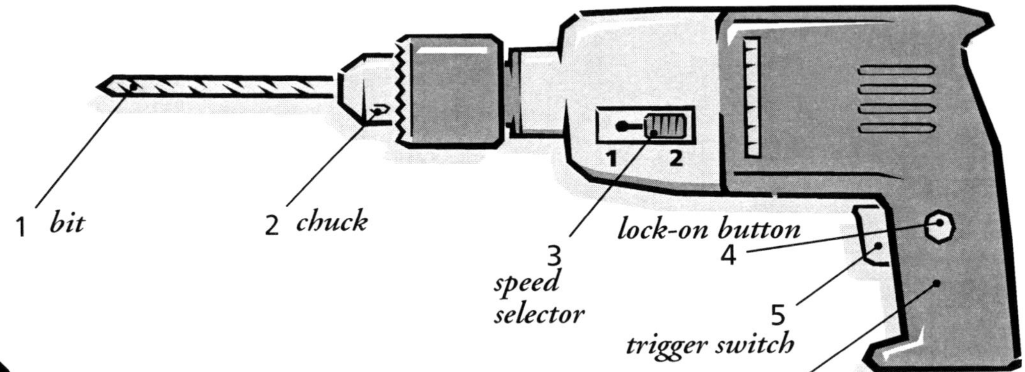

SAFETY
This drill is double insulated.
- Use the drill only with AC, correct voltage is 240.
- Don't use the drill in wet places.
- The cable must be in order.

AC	*alternating current*
DC	*direct current*

TRIGGER SWITCH
To work with the drill, you pull the trigger switch in the drill handle. For continuous operation you pull the trigger switch and press the 'lock-on-button' at the side of the switch. To stop continuous operation you only pull the trigger switch and release it afterwards.

to pull	*ziehen*
to release	*lösen*
to operate	*bewegen*

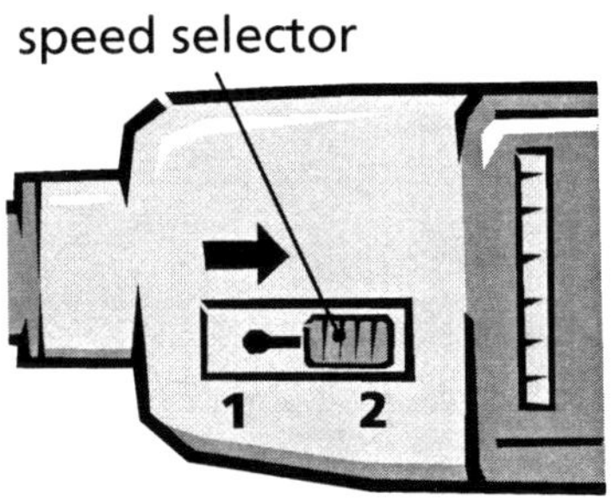

TWO SPEED SELECTOR
The drill has two speeds (1200 r.p.m. and 3000 r.p.m.) these are called high speed and low speed. To select the correct speed you push the switch in position 1 or 2 at the side of the drill.

to select	*wählen*

LOOSENING THE CHUCK
Only use the correct chuck key. Put the chuck key in the chuck. Turn the key anti-clockwise. If the key is tight, tap the key with a small hammer. To tighten the chuck again, turn the key clockwise.

to tap	*klopfen*
to tighten	*festigen*
to loosen	*lösen*

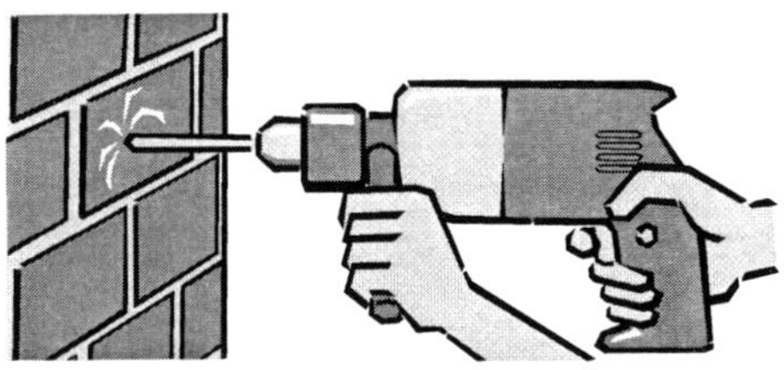

DRILLING
metal – use lubricant
wood – mark point of hole first, low speed
stone – use firm pressure, remove dust

Option
Tools and jobs – working with an electric drill

Lesson **1.2**

Finish the sentence.

1. To operate the drill, pull *the trigger switch.*
2. To select high speed, *push the switch in position two.*
3. To loosen the chuck, *turn the chuck key anti-clockwise.*
4. For continuous operation *press the lock-on button.*

Answer the questions.

5. What does the trigger switch do?

   It starts or stops the electric drill.

6. How many speeds does it have?

   The drill has high and low speed.

7. What is the correct voltage for this drill?

   It is 240 volts.

8. Can it drill iron and steel?

   Yes, of course it can.

9. When do you use high speed and when low speed?

   Low speed is for wood and large holes, high speed for small holes.

10. What switches are A and B and what are they used for?

    Switch A is used for speed selection,

    switch B is used for continuous operation.

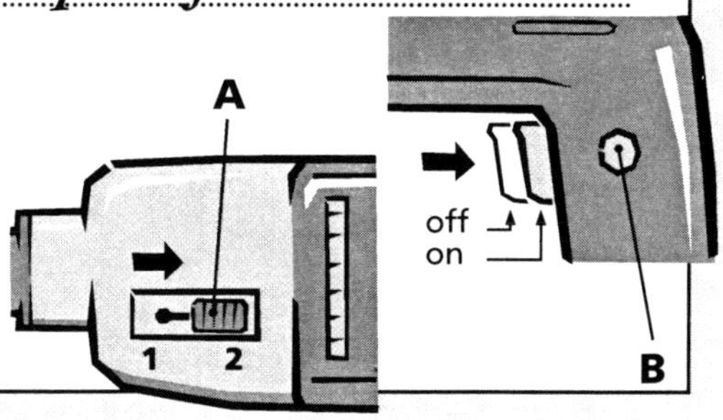

Right or wrong?	YES	NO
1. You can use the drill with AC and DC current.		*X*
2. To stop continuous operation you tap the trigger with a hammer.		*X*
3. It is possible to use the drill when it is wet.		*X*
4. You turn the key clockwise to loosen the chuck.		*X*
5. The correct voltage is 110 volts.		*X*
6. To tighten the chuck you use a chuck key.	*X*	
7. To operate the drill you press the trigger switch.	*X*	
8. You must use high speed for small holes.	*X*	
9. When drillling stone, press very hard.	*X*	

1.	The bottle is empty.	*Please, fill it.*
2.	The door is open.	*Please, close it.*
3.	The belt is tight.	*Please, loosen it.*
4.	The windows are open.	*Please, close them.*
5.	The screws are loose.	*Please, tighten them.*
6.	The bin is full.	*Please, empty it.*
7.	The pipe is too long.	*Please, cut it short.*
8.	The saw is on the floor.	*Please, pick it up.*
9.	The bottles are full.	*Empty them, please.*
10.	This piece of wood is too long.	*Cut it short, please.*
11.	The boxes are on the workbench.	*Put them down please.*
12.	The light is on.	*Switch it off, please.*
13.	The nails are everywhere.	*Put them in a box, please.*
14.	The machine is off.	*Turn it on, please.*
15.	I would like to start the machine.	*Press the button, please.*
16.	There are too many things on this workbench.	*Put them away, please.*

anti-clockwise, downwards, outwards, backwards, to the left, to the right.

a) to push *Push the lever to the right.*

b) to turn *Turn the key clockwise.*

c) to move *Move the car upwards*

d) to drive *Drive the car forwards.*

e) to bend *Bend the nails inwards.*

f) to push *Push the lever to the left.*

g) to turn *Turn the key anti-clockwise.*

h) to move *Move the car downwards.*

i) to drive *Drive the car backwards.*

j) to bend *Bend the nails outwards.*

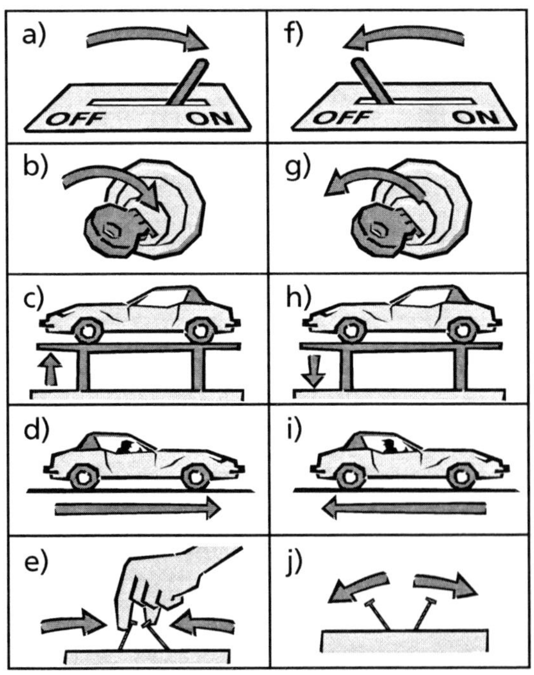

Instructions 2

Name the different jobs: Give instructions.

Electrician: Please put the wires into the wall!

a) Dig the foundations, please.

b) Build the wall.

c) Erect the roof.

d) Put the wires into the walls.

e) Install the pipes.

f) Plaster the walls.

g) Paint the walls.

a) construction worker

b) bricklayer

c) carpenter

d) electrician

e) plumber

f) mason

g) painter

Can you explain how a house is built?

First the *construction worker* makes the foundations. Then *the bricklayer builds the walls. Then the carpenter erects the roof. Next, the electrician puts all the wiring into the walls. Then the plumber installs all the pipes for fresh water and sewage. Then, again, the mason plasters the walls and smoothes them. Finally the painter sticks wall paper onto the walls and paints it afterwards. Then you can move in.*

Please translate.

1. *Please, pick the hammer up.*
2. *Undo the screw.*
3. *Fill the tank.*
4. *Please, press the button.*
5. *Close the door, please.*
6. *Please, smooth this piece of wood.*
7. *Push the lever to the right.*
8. *Pull the gear stick to the left.*
9. *Switch the light on.*
10. *Please, hammer this nail in.*
11. *Cut the wire, please.*
12. *Hold the iron with a pair of pliers, please.*

More instructions

1. Please give me the nails, Rick.
2. Can you give me the ruler please, Ahmed?
3. *Please, give me the pair of pliers.*
4. *Can you give me the goggles, please?*
5. *Please, give me the screwdriver.*
6. *Can you give me the helmet, please?*
7. *Please, pass me the hammer, Rick.*
8. *Can you pass me the saw, please?*
9. *Please, pass me the open spanner, Rick.*
10. *Please, give me the setquare.*
11. *Can you pass me the pincers, please?*
12. *Please, give me the pencil.*

The boss is really angry. Rick makes a lot of mistakes. He tells him what to do.

1. *Put the knife down.*
2. *Take the tie off.*
3. *Pick the chisels up.*
4. *Put the goggles on.*
5. *Extinguish the fag.*
6. *Use the protection shield.*
7. *Close the drawer.*
8. *Put the light on.*

All these instructions also work in their negative forms:
Don't wear a tie. Don't smoke. Don't work without the shield. ... etc.

More instructions

1. *Don't touch it, it's live.*
2. *Don't saw it, there's a nail.*
3. *Don't switch it on, there's no bulb.*
4. *Don't put them on, the glasses are broken.*
5. *Don't hit the nail, it's bent.*
6. *Don't pull it, there are bricks on it.*

Rick has his first driving-lesson. He tells the instructor what he wants to do. The instructor gives the following instructions:

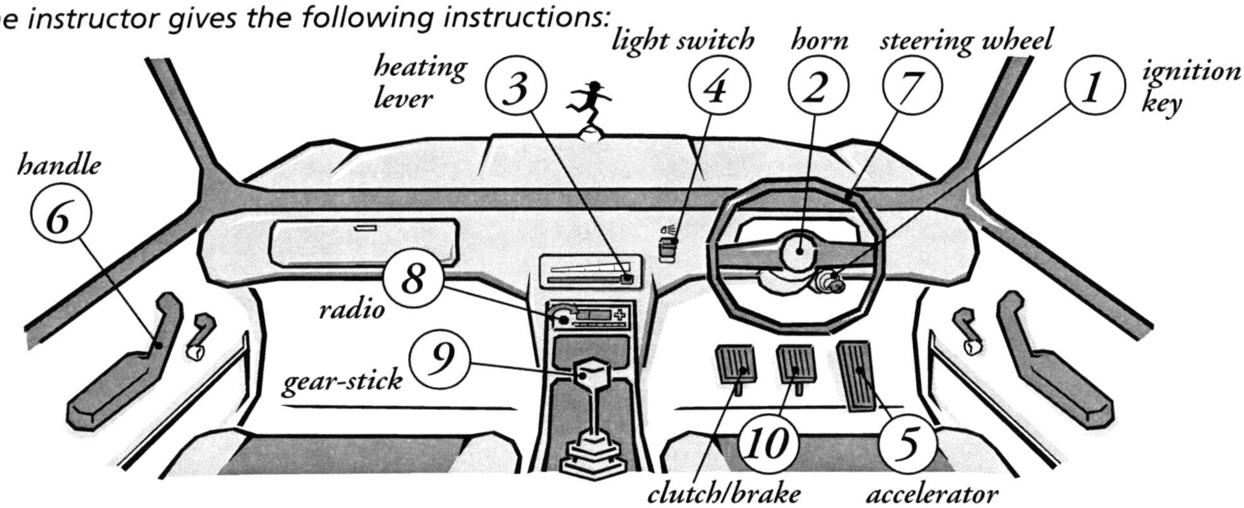

Rick says:	*The instructor answers:*
1. I would like to start the engine.	1. Turn the key clockwise.
2. I must give a signal.	*2. Press the horn.*
3. It is too hot for me inside.	*3. Turn the heating off.*
4. Now it is too dark outside.	*4. Switch the light on.*
5. I would like to go faster.	*5. Press the accelerator.*
6. My door is still open.	*6. Pull the handle.*
7. I would like to turn right.	*7. Move the steering wheel to the right.*
8. I would like some music.	*8. Turn the radio on.*
9. How can I go backwards?	*9. Put the gear into reverse.*
10. Now I must stop the car.	*10. Press the brake softly, please.*

Option 2

How many – plural and numbers

Lesson **1.3**

Find the plural of these tools and write them into the correct box.

file – files	switch – switches	battery – batteries	man – men
vice – vices *bottle – bottles* *bulb – bulbs* *table – tables* *tyre – tyres* *house – houses* *car – cars* *nail – nails*	*box – boxes*	*factory – factories*	*woman – women* *knife – knives* *a pair of glasses – two pairs of glasses*

Jason goes shopping.

a) pencils 4
b) knives 1
c) switches 3
d) bulbs 2
e) nails 20
f) screws 30
g) batteries ... 8
h) nuts 9
i) bolts 6
j) files 7

1

2

3

4

1. How many tyres are there? There are six.

2. There are four batteries.

3. There are eight switches.

4. There are many people.

5. There are five factories.

6. There are two boxes.

7. There are seven houses.

8. There are nine cars.

Also describe things in the classroom like: There are 20 students. There is one blackboard …

5

6

7

8

Option 3

Numbers

Lesson **1.3**

1. Read out the sums. Give answers.

13 + 18 =	900 – 34 + 59 =	144 : 12 =
24 – 11 =	78 x 7 + 64 =	1,800 – 89 =
77 x 12 =	90 : 2 =	1,000,000 : 500 =
555 – 10 x 7 =	22 x 22 =	235,890 – 3,890 =

2. Read out the task and solve them.

a) **Multiply** 98.4 by 5 and **divide** the answer by 12.
b) Add 33.5 to 26.35 and substract 45.8 from the answer.
c) Divide 40.5 by 5 and multiply the answer by 8.
d) **Add** 235.08 to 51.73 and **substract** the answer from 326.2.
e) Substract 54.63 from 85.01. Add 2.227. Substract the answer from 61.9

3. Go on with the sequence.

1, 3, 5, 7, *9, 11, 13, 15, 17* .... *odd numbers*

2, 4, 6, 8, *10, 12, 14, 16, 18* .... *even numbers*

3, 9, 81, ... *form squares*

105, 99, 93, 87, *81, 75, 69* .... *substract six*

2, 3, 8, 63, ... *double the number minus one*

4. Complete the table

Number	Word		Short form
1	one	first	1 st
2	*two*	*second*	*2 nd*
3	*three*	*third*	*3 rd*
4	*four*	*fourth*	*4 th*
5	*five*	*fifth*	*5 th*
6	*six*	*sixth*	*6 th*
7	*seven*	*seventh*	*7 th*
8	*eight*	*eighth*	*8 th*
9	*nine*	*ninth*	*9 th*
10	*ten*	*tenth*	*10 th*
11	*eleven*	*eleventh*	*11 th*
12	*twelve*	*twelvth*	*12 th*

a) Volume = ?

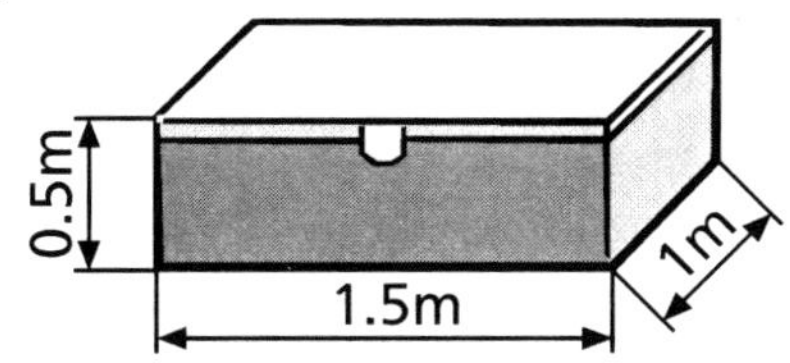

b) Volume = 21 m³ BC = ?

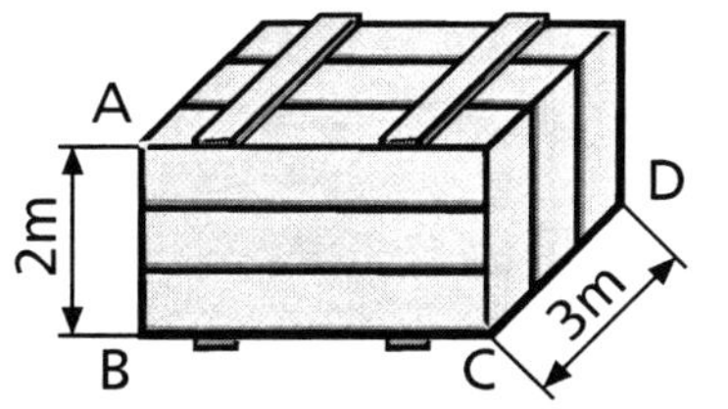

c) Height of house = ?

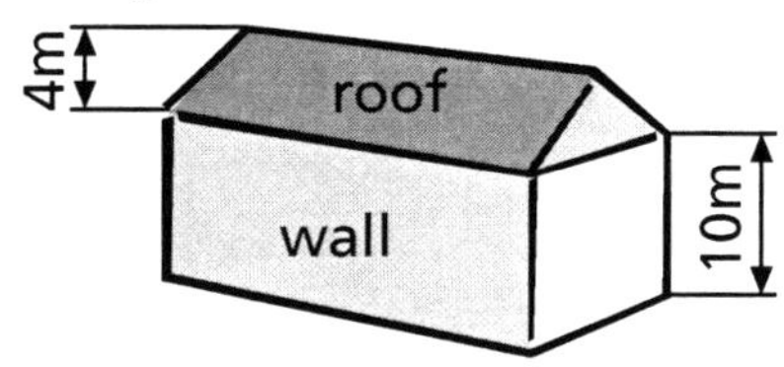

d) Height of tank = ?

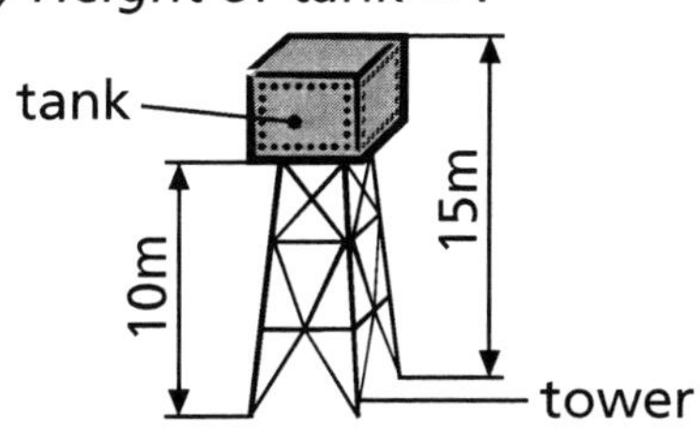

e) Volume of drawer = ?

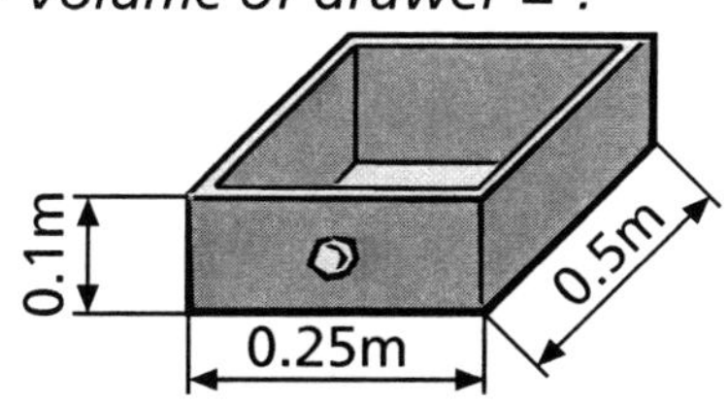

Revision unit (Lesson 1.0 - 1.3)
Page 1

Lesson **1.4**

							1	D	R	I	L	L					
	2	S	P	A	N	N	E	R									
					3	P	A	I	R	O	F	P	L	I	E	R	S
							4	V	I	C	E						
			5	S	A	N	D	E	R								
							6	B	R	U	S	H					
		7	S	I	D	E	C	U	T	T	E	R					
			8	P	A	I	N	T	I	N	G	R	O	L	L	E	R
9 C	R	O	S	S	H	E	A	D									
			10	M	I	C	R	O	M	E	T	E	R				
				11	S	P	A	N	N	E	R						
						12	C	O	M	P	A	S	S	E	S		
		13	M	A	L	L	E	T									
				14	C	O	L	D	C	H	I	S	E	L			
		15	H	A	M	M	E	R									
						16	P	I	N	C	E	R	S				
				17	P	L	A	N	E								
				18	H	A	C	K	S	A	w						

1. You can make a whole with a ...
2. You can tighten or loosen things with a ...
3. You can hold and cut things with a ...
4. You can hold small things in a ...
5. You can smooth things with ...
6. You can paint a window with a ...
7. You can cut cables with a ...
8. You paint walls with a ...
9. It is a special screwdriver.
10. You measure small things with it.
11. You can do up and undo nuts and bolts with a ...
12. You can draw circles with a pair of ...
13. It is a special hammer.
14. You can cut stones or bricks with it.
15. You can hit nails with a ...
16. You can pull out nails with it.
17. You can smooth wood with a ...
18. You can cut metal with a ...

Fill in the right verb!

1. It's cold outside, you must ....*close*.... the window.
2. To stop the machine, you must ....*press*.... the button.
3. At the petrol station you can ....*fill*.... your tank.
4. When I come home I ....*switch on*.... the radio.
5. You see 5 Euro on the street and ....*pick them up*....
6. When the film is over I ....*switch off*.... the video recorder.
7. My jeans are too wide I must ....*tighten*.... them with a belt.
8. If you are hungry ....*you open*.... the fridge.
9. My brother ....*hits/drives*.... the nail into the wall for the new picture.
10. The engine ....*pulls*.... 10 wagons.

to press
to switch off
to fill
to pick up
to close
to switch on
to tighten
to open
to hit
to pull

Revision unit (Lesson 1.0 - 1.3)

Page 2

Instructions.

1. I would like to drink a can of coke. *Give me a can, please.*
2. The room is dark. *Please, switch on the light.*
3. This piece of wood is too rough. *Smooth it, please.*
4. The screws are under the workbench. *Please, pick them up.*
5. Your walkman is on. *Turn it off, please.*
6. The nuts are undone. *Tighten them, please.*
7. The book is open. *Please, close it.*
8. The wire is too long. *Please, cut it short.*

to dig; construction worker

to lay; bricklayer

to build; carpenter

Please translate.

1. Der Elektroingenieur macht die Schaltpläne.
   The engineer makes the plans.
2. Der Zimmermann benutzt eine Feile.
   The carpenter uses a file.
3. Der Klempner bohrt ein Loch in das Rohr.
   The plumber drills a hole into the pipe.
4. Der Technische Zeichner braucht ein Lineal und Zirkel.
   The technical draughtsman needs a ruler and compasses.
5. Der Automechaniker löst die Schrauben mit einem Schraubenschlüssel.
   The car mechanic loosens the bolts with a spanner.
6. Dar Maler streicht die Wand.
   The painter paints the wall.

to wire; electrician

to fix; plumber

to smooth; mason

to paint; painter

Option 1

Crossword

Lesson **1.4**

1 F	I	L	E		2 T		3 T		4 T	E	E	5 N
L				6 L	A	B	E	L				U
A					P		N					T
7 P	A	8 P	E	R				9 C	A	10 S	E	S
		L			11 D		12 F			P		
13 B	E	A	K	E	R		14 I	S	M	A	D	E
		S			I		F			N		
15 P	E	T	R	O	L		16 T	W	E	N	T	Y
		I			L		H			E		
17 S	A	C	K	S				18 S	C	R	E	19 W
A					20 T		21 A					O
N				22 T	H	I	R	D				O
23 D	R	U	M		E		E		24 H	E	A	D

Across

1. 

4. 15 = fif …
   16 = six …

6. 

7. 

9. 

13. 

14. The container is a box.
    It … of metall.

15. 

16. 20 = …

17. 

18. 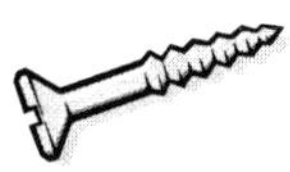

22. 3rd = …

23. 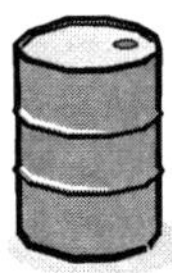

24. ? 

Down

1. 

2. 

3. 10 = …

5. 

8.  The handle is made of …

10. 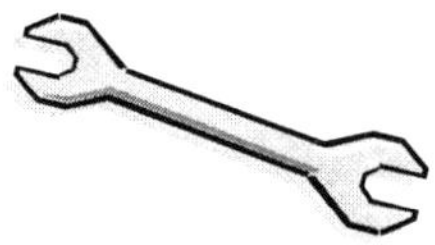

11. 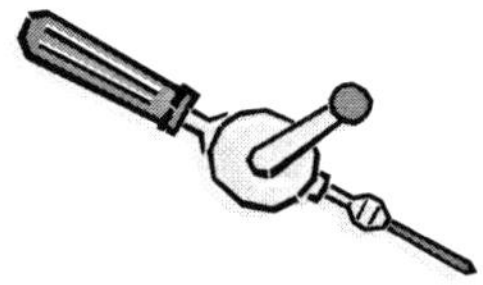

12. 5th = …

17. 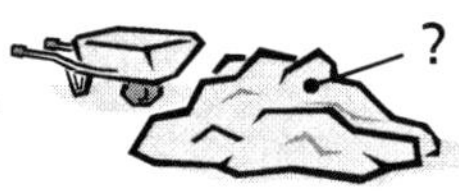

19. 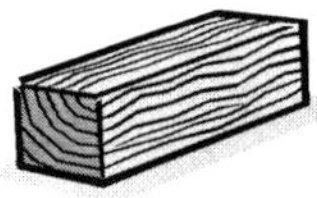

20. This tool is a hammer.
    … handle is made of wood.

21. These containers are boxes.
    They … made of wood.

Option 2

Crossword

1 B	L	U	E		2 S			3 A		
U					4 P	L	5 A	N	E	6 S
7 S	A	8 W			A		M			E
		H		9 I	N		E			E
	10 B	I	G		N		11 R	E	12 D	
13 B		T			E		I		E	
14 E	L	E	15 C	T	R	I	C	I	A	N
N			H				A		R	
16 T	17 A	X	I				18 N	O		
	R		S		19 S				20 I	21 S
22 T	E	L	E	P	H	O	N	E		A
			L		E					M

Across

1. A colour.

4. 

7. 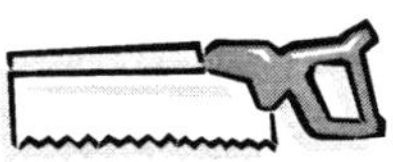

9. There´s a hammer … the tool-box.

10. Not small.

11. The colour of the television.

14. 

16. 

18. … , he isn´t.

20. Yes, it …

22. 

Down

1. 

2. 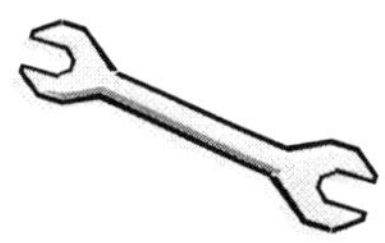

3. He´s … engineer.

5. Tom´s nationality.

6. 

8. Not black.

12. Oh … !

13. Not straight.

15. 

17. Yes, they …

19. Yes, … is

21. 

Where is it? 1 – prepositions

Lesson **1.5**

1. The rope is *around* the tree.
2. The tree is *next* to the house.
3. The cat is *under* the table.
4. The plane is *over* the house.
5. The mouse is *in* the vase.
6. The mouse is *inside* the box.
7. Rick walks *across* the river.

8. Jason is resting *against* the wall.
9. The baby is sitting *on* the table.
10. Duncan is sitting *on* a chair *at* the table.
11. The tree is *between* the two houses.
12. Rick is drilling *through* the wall.
13. Ahmed is walking *along* the road.
14. Ron is standing *among* the trees.

Where is it? 2 – prepositions Lesson 1.5

14. One tree is *in front* the other tree is *behind*.

15. The jogger first ran *up* the hill and later *down* the hill.

16. In my holidays I went *from* Bristol *to* Rome.

17. Rick can only speak to his girl friend from *outside*. Susan is standing *inside*.

18. The mouse jumps *out of* the box while the cat is jumping *into* it.

19. The cat jumps *onto* the table, but the mouse jumps *off* the table.

Try to translate these expressions:

im Haus *in the house*

unter dem Tisch *under the table*

auf dem Schrank *on the wardrobe*

zwischen den Zangen *between the pliers*

neben dem Hammer *next to the hammer*

über dem Schalter *above the switch*

über die Straße *across the road*

in der Schachtel *in the box*

in dem Glas *in the glass*

zwischen den Nägeln *between the nails*

gegen die Wand *against the wall*

vor der Werkbank *in front of the bench*

hinter der Maschine *behind the machine*

innerhalb der Fabrik *within the factory*

in die Schachtel hinein *into the box*

von Berlin nach Paris *from … to*

den Berg hinauf *up the hill*

die Straße hinunter *down the road*

Where is it? 3 – prepositions

Lesson **1.5**

1. The screwdriver is … *on the shelf*
   The board is … *at the wall*

2. The door is … *to the right of the switch.*
   The table is … *to the left of the socket.*
   The socket is … *between both*

3. The ruler is …
   in the drawer.

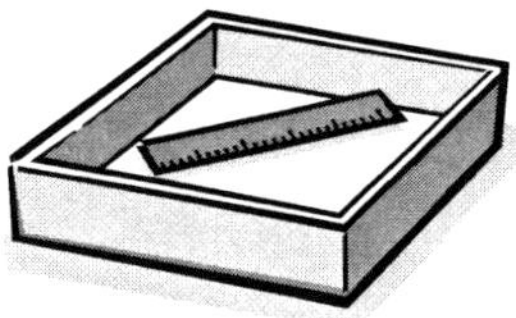

4. The switch is …
   above the table.
   The table is …
   below the switch.

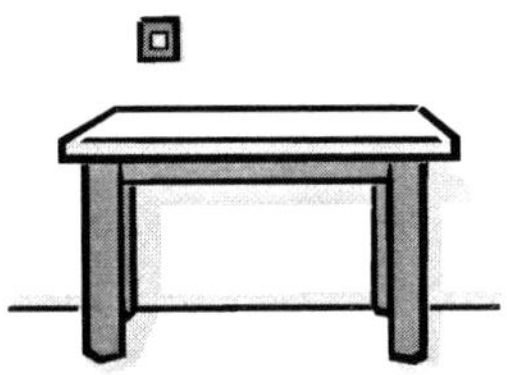

5. The box … *is under the table.*
   The table …
   is over the box.

6. The socket … *is below the window.*
   The window …
   is above the socket.

7. The screw …
   is in the box

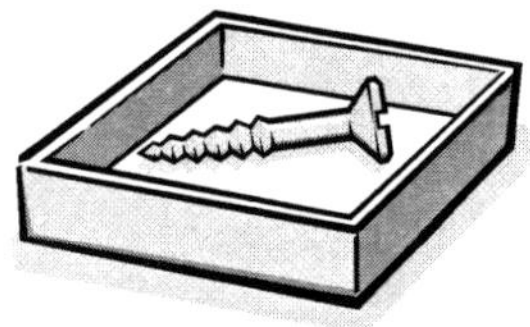

Now answer your neighbour the same way!

8. *Where is the fan?*
   It is between table and lamp.

9. *Where is the ruler?*
   It is on the chair.

10. *Where is the fan?*
    It is next to the door.

11. *Where is the saw?*
    It is under the board.

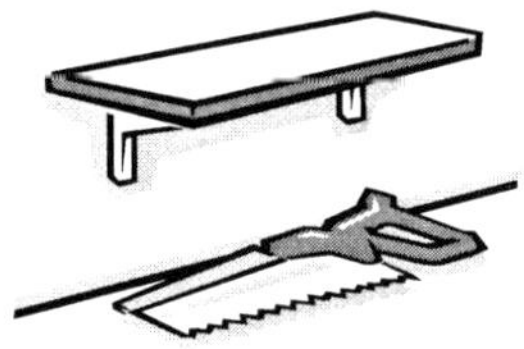

12. *Where is the socket?*
    It is above the table.

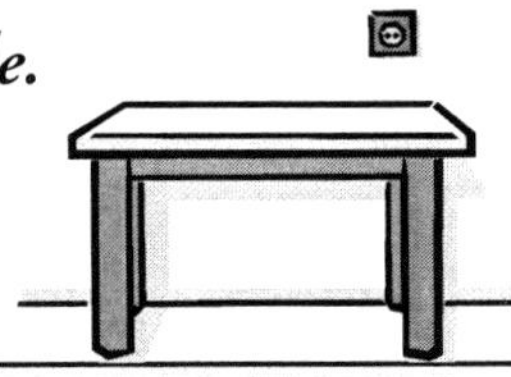

Describe the location of the tools in correct sentences.
Use: to the right, to the left, between, among, next to

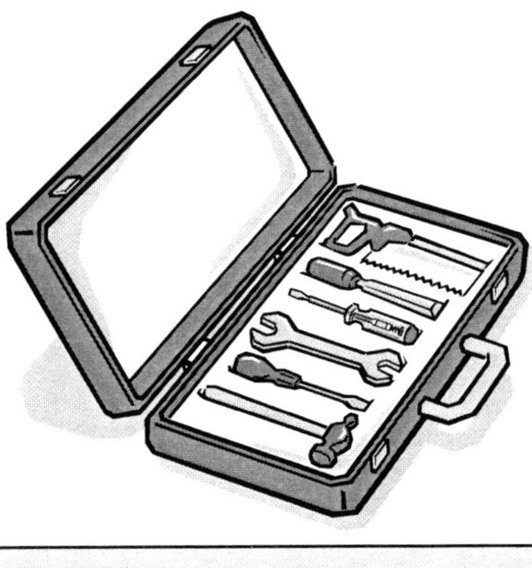

The saw is to the right of the chisel.
The (screwdriver) mains tester is to the left of the chisel.
The spanner is between screwdriver and mains tester.
Among these tools is a hammer.
Next to the saw is a chisel.

Many more excercises with things in the classroom possible.

Where is it? 4 – prepositions

Lesson **1.5**

Where is the hammer? — *It is on the wardrobe.*
Where are the nails? — *They are on the floor.*
Where are the spanners? — *They are in the drawer.*
Where is the pair of scissors? — *It is on the board.*
Where is the helmet? — *It is on the table* *(many more possible)*

How many nails are on the table?
How many windows are in the workshop?
How many nails are on the table?
How many saws are there?
How many spanners are in the workshop?

What is on the wardrobe? — *A hammer.*
What is on the table? — *A helmet, six nails and a ruler.*
What's on the floor? — *A saw, a pair of goggles, some nails.*
What's on the rack? — *A drill, a screwdriver, a chisel, a saw, a hammer and an open spanner.*

The boss is not pleased with the mess in the workshop.
He tells Rick what to do. Give instructions.

Pick the screws up.
Put the nails in the box.
Pick the saw up.
Don't be lazy.
Put the helmet on.
Open the window.
Put the goggles on.
Start work.
Don't behave like a child.
Close the drawer.

What are they doing? 1 – simple and continuous Lesson **1.6**

Every day Mr. Smith smokes 30 cigarettes.
Now he is smoking his last one.

Saturdays Peter and Sally go to the cinema.
Now they are going to a restaurant.

Normally Mrs. Hunter leaves the house at 8 o'clock.
Today she is leaving the house at 7.

Usually I get up at six o'clock.

Today I am staying in bed, because it's Sunday.

Write in the little words that show you what form to use!

Simple form	*Continuous form*
every day, normally *every week, Saturdays* *usually*	*today, now,* *at the moment*

1. The plumber (to drill) *drills* holes in pipes.
2. The elctrician (to bend) *bends* cables.
3. The drivers (to start) *start* the cars.
4. *Usually I go home at seven.*
5. *Normally I eat 5 hamburgers.*
6. *Water boils at 100 °C*

1. At this moment the teacher (to come) *is coming in*
2. Now the painter (to paint) *is painting* our flat.
3. The car mechanic (to test) *is testing* my car today.
4. *I'm listening to you now.*
5. *I'm eating a pizza.*
6. *The water is boiling. Get the tea mashed.*

What are these people doing?

is walking

are sleeping

is watching

is washing

is swimming

is standing

is listening

is brushing

is sitting

is reading

What are they doing? 2 – simple and continuous Lesson 1.6

9.00 *work in company*
At a quarter past nine Rick is not working in the company he is sleeping in bed.

English sports: rugby, cricket, baseball, soccer, hockey

11.45 *have lunch* *At a quarter to twelve Rick is not having lunch he is still sleeping.*

14.45 *clean workshop*

At a quarter to three Rick is not cleaning his workshop he is playing soccer

15.00 *have tea* *At three o'clock Rick is not having tea he is playing baseball.*

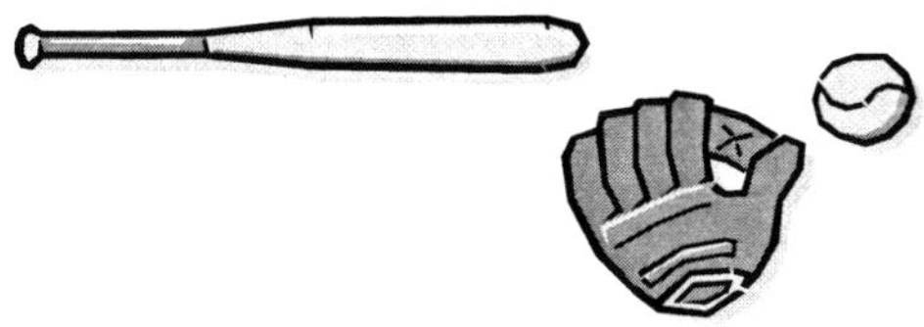

16.15 *leave work*
At a quarter past four Rick is not leaving work

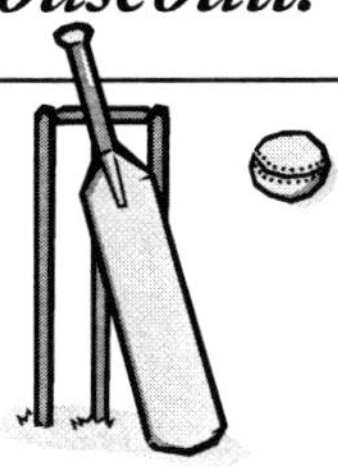

he is playing cricket.

17.00 *study at night school*
At five o'clock Rick is not studying at night school he is chatting with the girls.

18.25 *learn computer programming*
At twenty five past six Rick is not learning computer programming he is playing rugby.

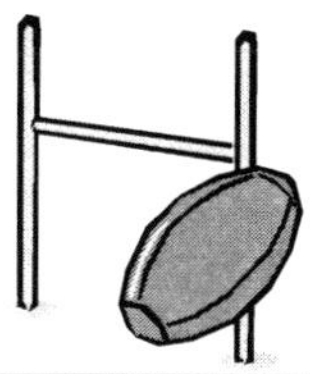

20.00 *finish night school*

At eight o'clock Rick is not finishing night school he is playing hockey.

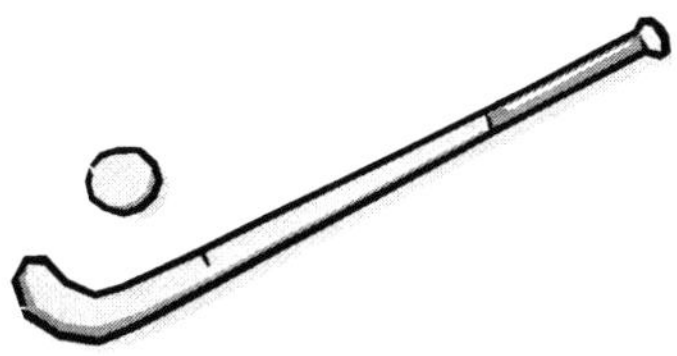

20.25 *meet Janet at the "Red Lion"*
At twenty-five past eight Rick is not meeting Janet he is completely shattered.

23.40 *watch television*

At twenty to twelve Rick is not watching tv he is sound asleep.

Now talk about Rick's normal working day:
Normally Rick works in the company at nine ...

How high is it? 1 – comparison of adjectives Lesson 1.7

1. **Jason** weighs 70 kilograms.
2. He is 1.80 metres tall.
3. He is 40 years old and single.
4. He smokes 25 cigs a day.
5. He has a Mercedes and a Mini.

1. **Ahmed** weighs 75 kilograms.
2. He is 1.87 metres tall.
3. He is 25 years old and married. He has a son and three daughters.
4. He smokes two packets of Marlboro.
5. He has got a Rover.

1. **Rick** weighs 60 kilos.
2. He is 1.75 metres tall.
3. He is 17 years old and has a nice girl friend.
4. He does not smoke but drinks 5 pints of Newcastle Brown Ale every night.
5. He has got a motorbike and a bicycle.

1. **Duncan** weighs 82 kilos.
2. He is 1.95 metres tall.
3. He is 58 years old, married and has three children.
4. He smokes cigars and drinks two pints of Guinness every night.
5. He has got three cars in his family.

Form sentences like this: Duncan is **heavier** than Rick.
Use: taller, lighter, heavier, more, less, older, younger, bigger, smaller, taller

Jason is smaller than Ahmed.

Ahmed is taller than Rick.

Rick is younger than Duncan.

Rick drinks more beer than Duncan.

The boss is the tallest.

Ducan has most cars in his family.

Ahmed is the worst smoker in the workshop.

Duncan is the heaviest of them all.

Rick is not the tallest of them all. (...)

How high is it? 2 – comparison of adjectives

Lesson **1.7**

1. *Complete the list.*

	Type 1 (short words)	
long	*longer*	*longest*
high	*higher*	*highest*
wide	*wider*	*widest*
thick	*thicker*	*thickest*
deep	deeper	deepest
heavy	heavier	heaviest
big	bigger	biggest
small	***smaller***	***smallest***
rich	***richer***	***richest***
	Type 2 (long words)	
expensive	more expensive	most expensive
beautiful	*more beautiful*	*most beautiful*
interesting	*more interesting*	*most interesting*
	Type 3 (irregular)	
good	*better*	*best*
bad	*worse*	*worst*
little	*less*	*least*
many / ***much***	*more*	*most*

2. *Form sentences.* The wall is **longer than** the wire.

a)

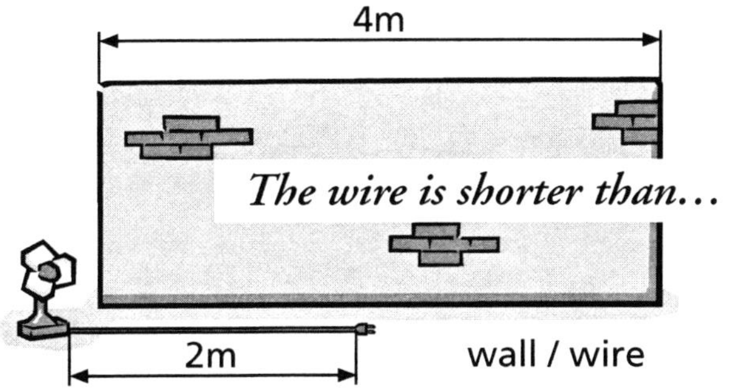

wall / wire

c)

b)

truck / bridge

d)

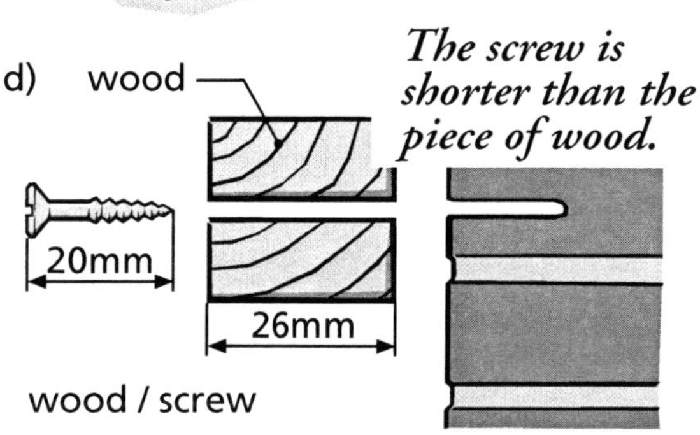

wood / screw

t	o	w	a	r	d	s		b			o	u	t	s	i	d	e	
	v				o		n	e	a	r								
	e				w			l							b	o	n	
	r				n			o	p	p	o	s	i	t	e			
b	e	h	i	n	d			w				i			t			
				a	b	o	v	e				n	a		w	i	t	h
	a			m	t	h	r	o	u	g	h	s	t		e		t	o
	c	a	l	o	n	g	a			b	y	i			e			
a	r	o	u	n	d		b					d		u	n	d	e	r
	o			g			o		a	f	t	e	r	p			Ü	
	s						u											
	s						t		a	g	a	i	n	s	t			

1. *Spot these prepositions in the table above. Form two teams in class.*
   Ready! Steady! Go!

towards over above below opposite between among with around under near by at	running mechanic  team 1	outside on inside along after through up down across about against to behind	reading boss  team 2

2. *Compare both pictures.*
   Ask and answer questions like this: "Where is Jason?

   "He is under the workbench."

1. Where are the screws?
2. Where is the chair?
3. Where is the vice?
4. What is on the table?
5. Who is under the table?

"He is in front of the table."

1. They are on the table.
2. It is in front of the table.
3. It is at the table.
4. The screws and nothing else.
5. Lazy Jason, of course.

1.		*The saw is between the hammer and screwdriver.*	5.		*There are three tools on the rack.*
2.	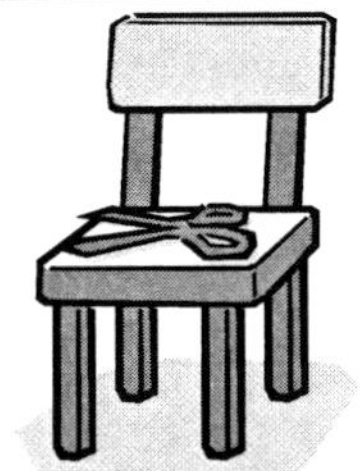	*The pair of scissors is on the chair.*	6.	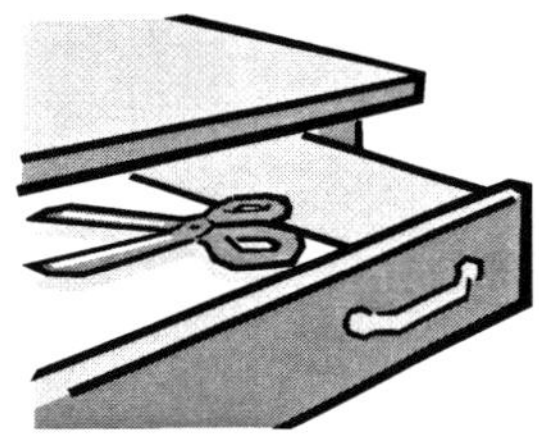	*The pair of scissors is in the drawer.*
3.		*The saw is on the board.*	7.		*The saw is at the wall.*
4.	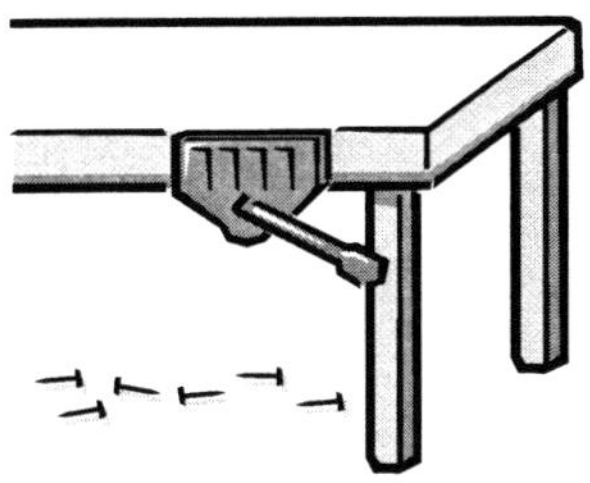	*The vice is at the table. The nails are under the table.*	8.	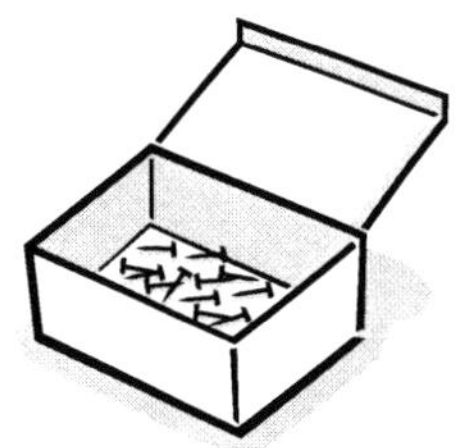	*The nails are in the box.*

3. Describe what Mr. Lucky is doing in each individual picture. (Continuous Form)
Then tell the story of Mr. Lucky's unlucky day. (Remember to use the correct prepositions.)

Story starts like this: (Present Tense) *One day Mr. Lucky sleeps quietly next to his wife. He sits around the table for breakfast. Then he speaks …*

Revision unit (Lesson 1.5 - 1.7) Lesson 1.8
Page 3

4. Use the -ing form or simple form where necessary.

Ann (to go, normally) *normally goes* to school by bus. Today she (to use) *is using* her father's car. At the bus stop she (to see) *sees* her friends, she (to stop) *stops* the car and (to give) *gives* them a lift. In the car they (to talk) *are talking* about the disco last night, their new teachers and the trouble at work. Ann (to like) *likes* her job very much, but she (to hate) *hates* her day at school and the stupid lessons there. They (to arrive) *arrive* at school just in time and at 9 o'clock sharp they (to sit) *are sitting* in the classroom and (to listen) *listening* to their favourite teacher Mr. Spock.

5. Complete this form!

positive	*comparative*	*superlative*
1. *good*	better	*best*
2. *bad*	*worse*	worst
3. many	*more*	*most*
4. *little*	*less*	least
5. *heavy*	heavier	*heaviest*
6. high	*higher*	*highest*

6. Please translate!

1. John ist älter als Nigel.
2. Nigel ist größer als Jack.
3. Jack ist schlauer als John.
4. Eisen ist schwerer als Aluminium.
5. Die Elbe ist breiter als die Spree.
6. Stahnsdorf ist kleiner als Berlin.

1. John is older than Nigel.

2. Nigel is taller than Jack.

3. Jack is cleverer than John.

4. Iron is heavier than aluminium.

5. The river Elbe is wider than the Spree.

6. Stahnsdorf is smaller than Berlin.

7. Life outside school is more interesting than inside.

Crossword

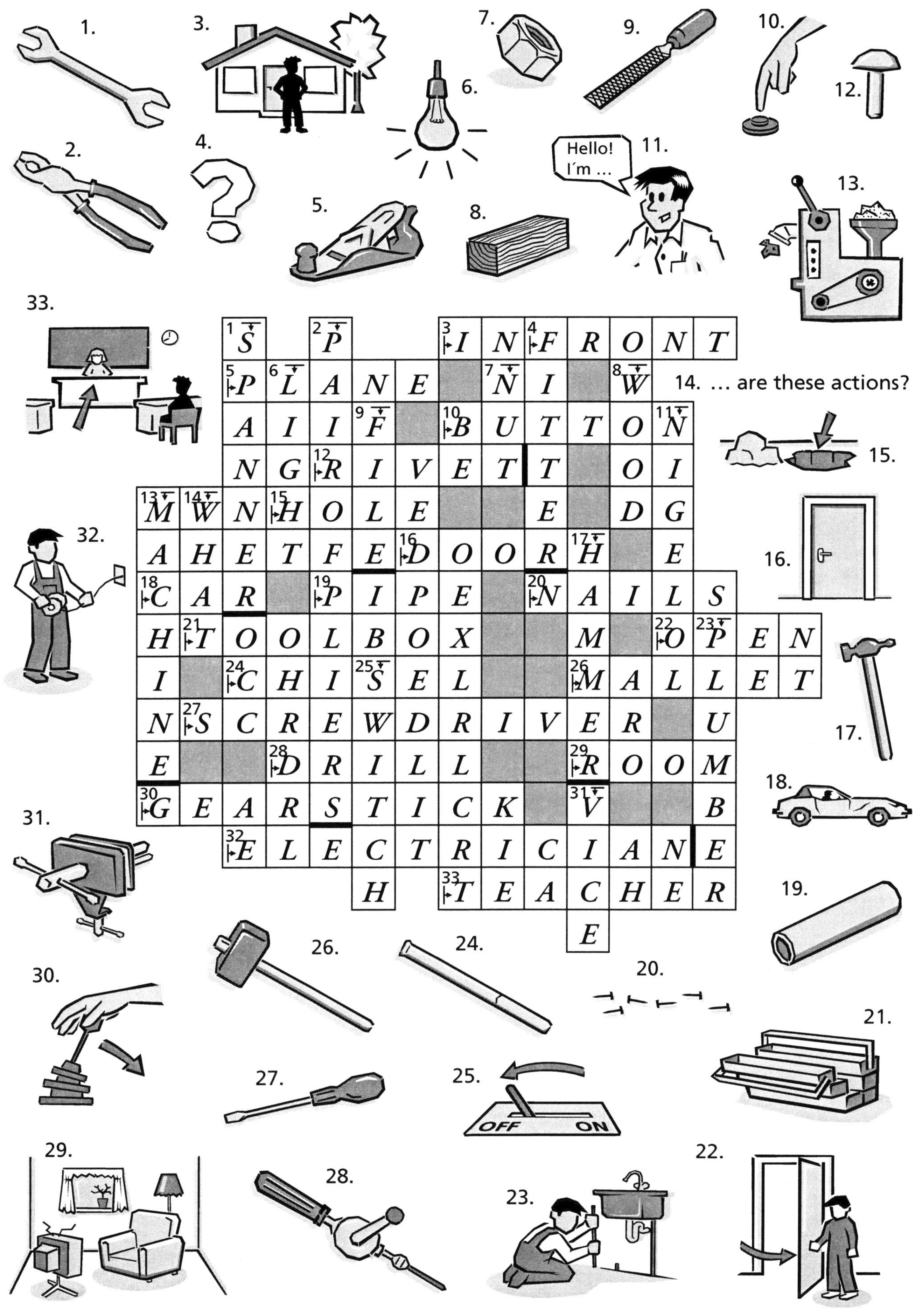

Materials and objects

Lesson **2.0**

1. Write down the materials of these objects and their names.

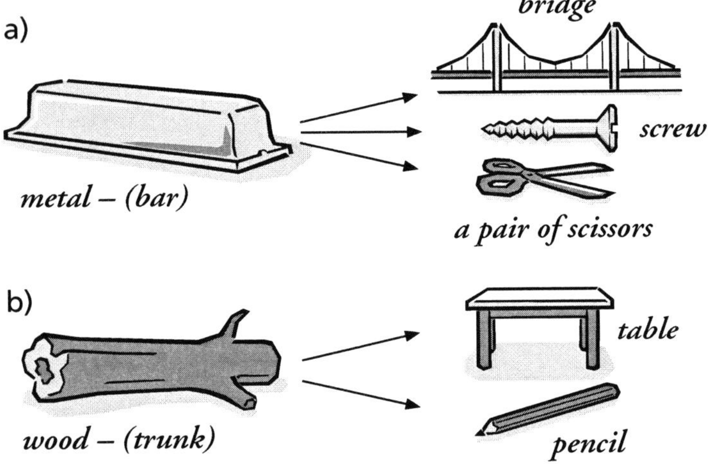

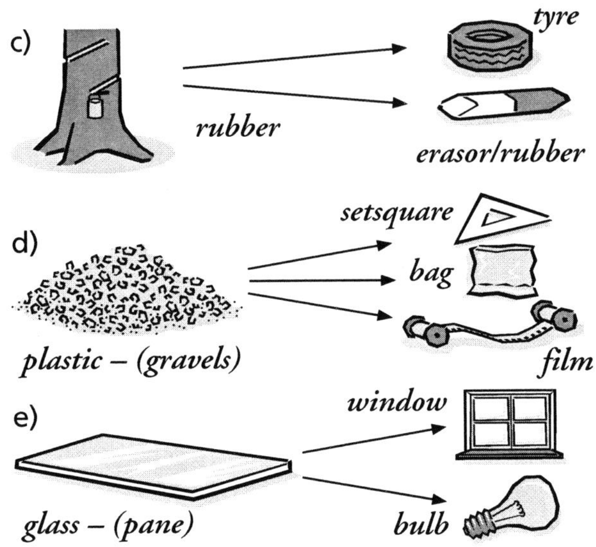

2. What are the objects made of?

"What is the setsquare made of?" "It's made of plastic."

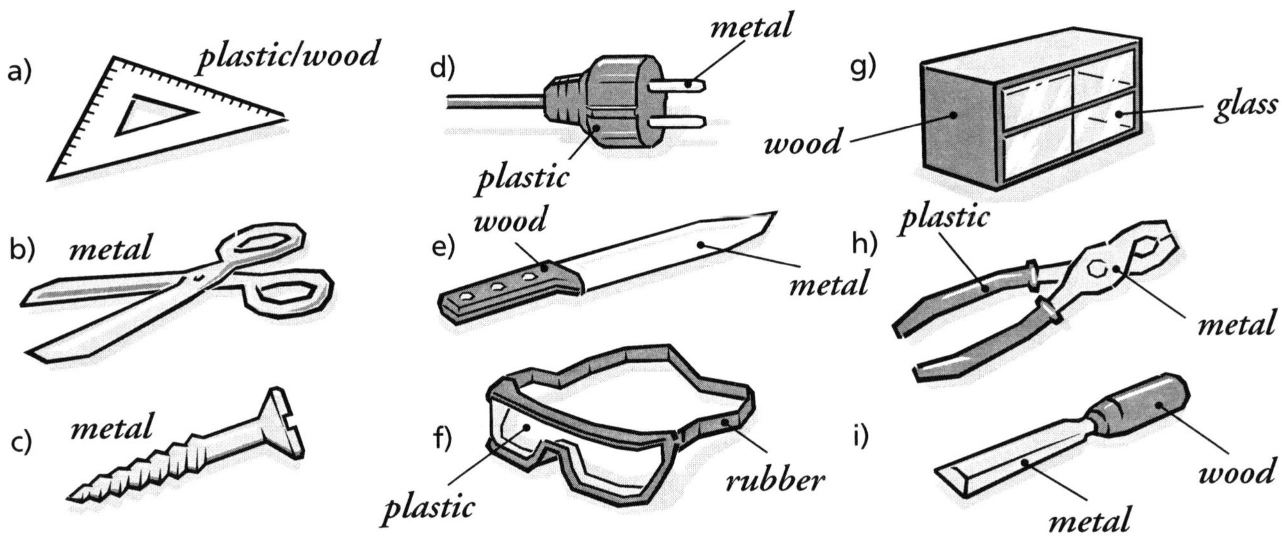

What's the plug made of? *It's made of metal and plastic.*

What's the window made of? *It's made of glass and wood.*

(...)

OPTIONAL:

1. How is metal produced? *By extracting oil from the earth and melting.*

2. How is wood produced? *By cutting trees.*

3. How is rubber produced? *By cutting rubber trees and collecting its milk.*

4. How is glass produced? *By melting sand.*

Materials and properties

Lesson **2.0**

1. *Complete the table. Then answer the questions and give reasons.*
   Start like this: Why are houses so tough? Because they are made of stone or concrete.
   Why are pipes made of copper? Because you can bend them easily.
   Why … Because … ***Go on!***

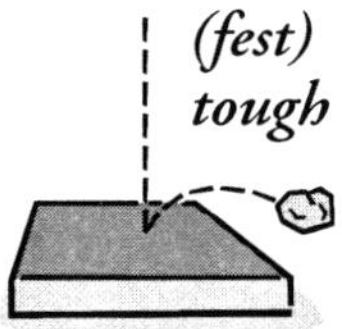

	material	*object*	*property*
1.	steel	*hammer*	tough
2.	stone	*wall*	*rigid*
3.	copper	*wire*	*flexible*
4.	concrete	*bridge*	*hard, tough*
5.	oil	*plastics*	*flammable*
6.	wood	*table*	*tough*
7.	glass	*window pane*	*transparent*
8.	paper	*book*	*light*
9.	plastic	*bag*	*light*
10.	rubber	*tyre*	*tough*
11.	iron	*file*	*rigid*

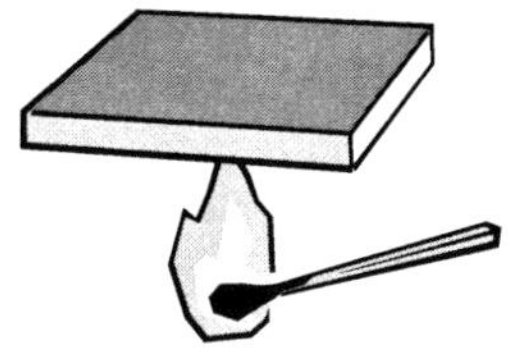

"Can you scratch a pane of glass easily?"
"No you can't. Glass is a hard material."
or "Yes, you can. Glass is quite smooth."

to bend to scratch
to burn to break

1. Can you bend a plank of wood easily?
   Yes, you can. Wood is quite flexible.
2. Can you bend a rubber tyre easily?
   Yes, you can. Rubber is quite flexible.
3. Can you burn a stone block easily?
   No, you can't. Stones are non-combustible.
4. Can you bend a concrete beam easily?
   No, you can't. Concrete is very rigid.
5. Can you burn a sheet of paper easily?
   Yes, you can. Paper is very combustible.
6. Can you bend iron easily?
   Yes, you can. When hot iron is very soft.

OPTION: *Why is wire made of copper?* *Because it is quite flexible.*
Why are bridges made of concrete? *Because concrete is very tough.*

Properties – some more properties

Lesson **2.1**

It is important to know the properties of engineering materials. For example, steel is used for making girders (1) because it is an elastic material. Cast iron (2) is never used for making girders because it is brittle. The properties of a material determine its use.

1. Malleability:
It is easy to roll malleable material into a new shape. A malleable material does not fracture easily under pressure.

2. Ductility:
It is easy to draw a ductile material. It does not fracture and it retains its new shape.

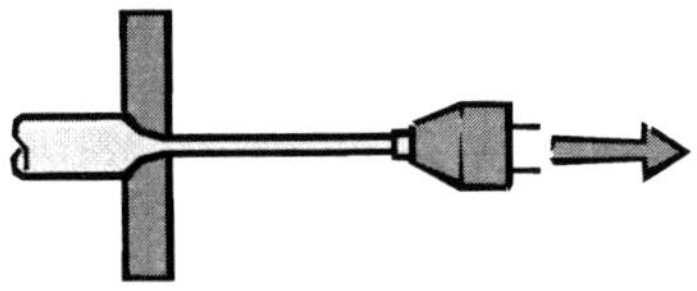

3. Elasticity:
An elastic material stretches easily under stress. If you remove the stress, it does not retain its shape. It regains its original shape.

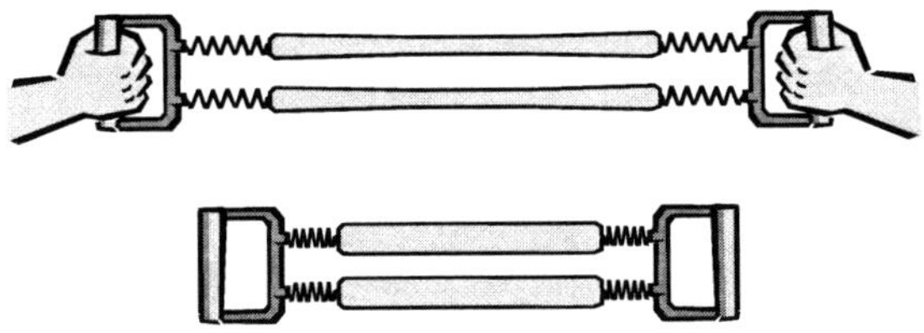

4. Durability:
A durable material does not corrode easily.

1. Girders = Stahlträger, 2. cast iron = Gußeisen., 3. to draw = hier: ziehen, 4. to retain = behalten

Material	Malleabilitiy	Ductility	Elasticity	Durability
Copper	•••••	•••••		••••
Aluminium	•••	••••		•••
Gold	•••••	••••		•••
Glass	•	•		•
Cast Iron	•	•	•	••••
Tin	••••	••••		••••
Steel	•••	••	•••	••
Lead	••••	••	••••	•••
Rubber			•••••	
Chromium	•••	•••		•••••
Platinum				•••••

extremely = ••••• very = •••• quite = ••• not very = •• not at all = •

Task: Compare the properties of these materials:

Examples: Gold is **more** malleable **than** aluminium.

Copper is the **most** ductile material.

Cast iron is **as** elastic **as** glass.

Steel is **not as** malleable **as** tin.

NOUN		*ADJECTIVE*
malleability	–	*malleable*
ductility	–	*ductile*
elasticity	–	*elastic*
durability	–	*durable*
flexibility	–	*flexible*
rigidity	–	*rigid*
	–	*brittle*
hardness	–	*hard*

Properties – some more properties

Lesson **2.1**

Write down 6 sentences made from the information given in the above table.
Use the words given, (page 36).

1. *Copper is* more *ductile* than *chromium.*
2. *Gold is one of* the most *expensive metals.*
3. *Steel is* as *ductile* as *lead.*
4. *Lead is* not as *elastic* as *rubber.*
5. *Cast iron is* more *durable* than *glass.*
6. *Rubber is* the most *elastic material of all.*

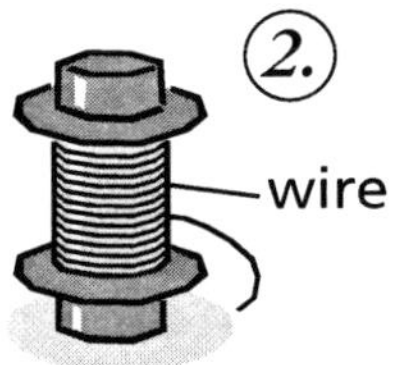

copper - ductile

steel - elastic

gold - expensive *(not)*

rubber - elastic

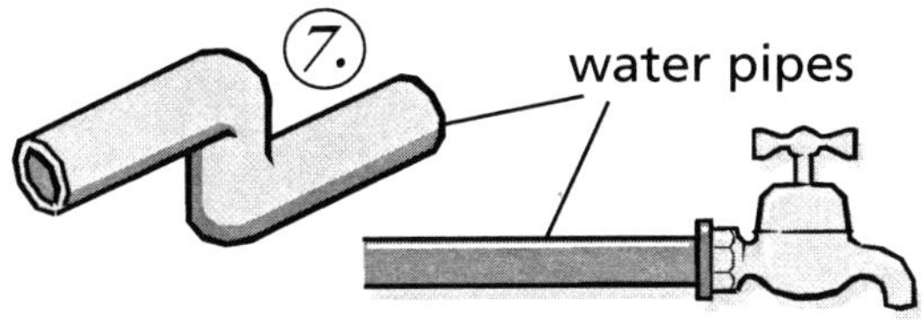

brass - durable

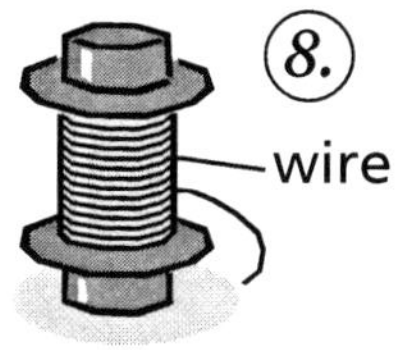

lead - brittle *(not)*

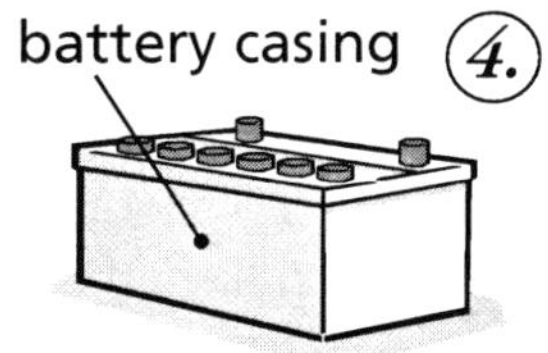

plastic - durable

Make sentences as follows:

1. Cast iron is not used for making girders because it is brittle.
2. *Copper is used for making wires because it is ductile.*
3. Springs *are made of steel because it is very elastic.*
4. Battery casings *are made of plastic because it is durable.*
5. *Gold is (not) used for electrical equipment because it is too expensive.*
6. *Rubber is used for fan belts because it is elastic.*
7. *Brass is used for water pipes because it is quite durable.*
8. *Lead is (not) used for wires because it is brittle. (two-style sentences)*

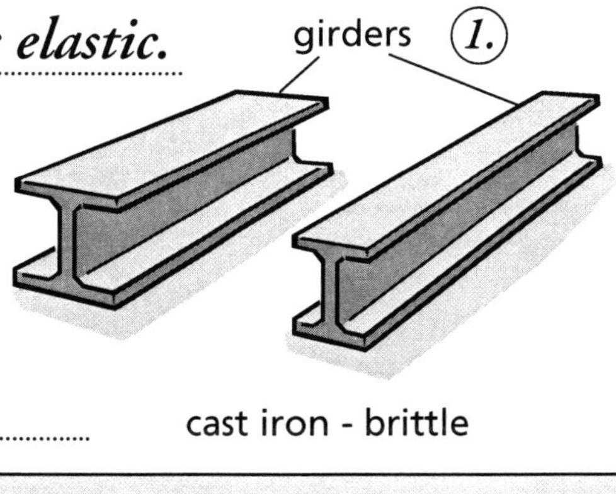

cast iron - brittle

Option 1

More materials, objects, properties

Lesson **2.1**

1. In this wordsnake you find things made of metal.
List them up and give German meanings.

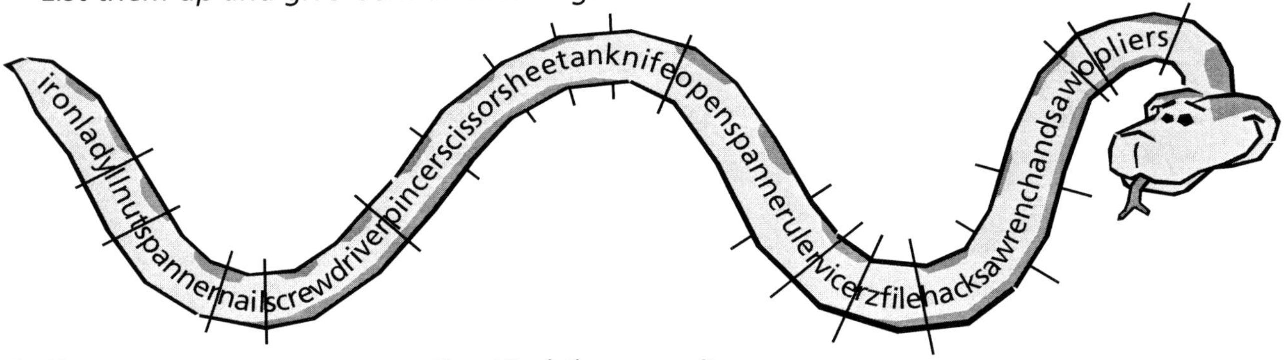

2. Here are some more properties. Find the opposites.

1. smooth *rough*	9. similar *different*
2. strong *weak*	10. new *old*
3. round *square*	11. loose *tight*
4. rusty *new*	12. long *short*
5. sharp *blunt*	13. rapid *slow*
6. short *tall / long*	14. fast *slow*
7. tall *small / little*	15. wet *dry*
8. thick *thin*	16. bent *even / straight*

3. In this box there is a real mess.
Put the words into the correct section.

palm, brass, copper, steel, plank, electric drill, silver, cast iron, rubber, pens, table, necklace, bridge, plastic, books, wires, titan, wedding rings, pine, screws, pliers, glass, bridge, lead, gold, goggles, aluminium, paper, insulation, concrete, marble, nuts, oak, granite, pebble, condoms, iron, discs, cupboards, chestnut tree, straps, houses, boxes, window panes, springs, casings, girders, workbench, helmet	**Metals:** *brass, copper, steel, silver, cast iron, titan, lead, gold, aluminium, iron*	**Items:** *electric drill, necklace, bridge, wedding rings, screws, pliers, nuts, discs, springs, girders*
	Wood: *palm, pine, oak, chestnut tree*	*plank, pen, table, cupboard, boxes, houses, casings, workbench*
	Others: *rubber, plastic, paper, glass, concrete, marble, granite, pebble*	*books, goggles, condom, straps, window, panes, helmet*

Now, sentence types from pages 35 and 37 are possible with the information given in this box.

Search-a-word

Everything made of ***plastic****.*
Write down the correct number of the English word.

1. basin	16. fork	a) Ornament 22	p) Becher 3
2. beads	17. handle	b) Schuhe 29	q) Isolierung 18
3. beaker	18. insulation	c) Platte 26	r) Tasche 9
4. bookends	19. knife	d) Einband 13	s) Krug 24
5. bowl	20. lens	e) Geschirr 14	t) Messer 19
6. box	21. necklace	f) Wasserbehälter 1	u) Griff 17
7. bracelet	22. ornament	g) Halsband, Kette 21	v) Kleid 15
8. button	23. pail	h) Perle, Wulst 2	w) Platte 30
9. case	24. pitcher	i) Stab, Stange 27	x) Stuhl 10
10. chair	25. place met	j) Bücherstütze 4	y) Linse 20
11. clothing	26. plate	k) Gabel 16	z) Mantel 12
12. coat	27. rod	l) Kugel 5	aa) Kleidung 11
13. cover	28. saucer	m) Kiste 6	bb) Eimer, Kübel 23
14. dishes	29. shoes	n) Untertasse 28	cc) Armband 7
15. dress	30. sheet	o) Platzdecke 25	dd) Knopf 8

Then spot them in this table.
There are six more items hidden in this table all starting with "s" or "t".

1. skirt / 2. spoon / 3. table
4. toy
5. tray
6. tube

Z	N	O	I	T	A	L	U	S	N	I	D	P	B	W	C	A
A	A	C	Y	G	M	R	P	K	J	O	B	L	U	B	L	L
D	X	M	O	E	T	A	J	N	O	J	V	A	T	O	O	Q
H	X	M	T	A	I	L	R	I	F	S	T	T	T	T	T	F
S	K	S	H	L	T	G	O	F	I	N	G	E	O	A	H	N
P	D	T	J	T	K	U	D	E	E	S	K	Y	N	B	I	M
O	R	R	U	T	Y	T	Q	M	B	U	F	K	R	L	N	E
O	E	E	N	B	F	A	A	A	K	E	S	A	C	E	G	H
N	S	H	L	S	E	N	R	R	C	F	C	R	Y	W	M	A
R	S	C	R	E	R	K	O	T	F	E	T	R	I	K	S	M
W	U	T	E	O	N	F	J	F	L	C	H	A	N	D	L	E
D	P	I	V	K	S	S	Z	E	B	P	B	S	K	N	V	Y
N	L	P	O	C	S	A	T	R	H	A	E	E	J	M	S	S
E	A	W	C	H	H	V	U	V	E	H	S	E	A	D	N	X
C	C	S	S	A	E	Z	H	C	S	K	S	I	N	D	O	X
K	E	W	E	I	E	O	V	I	E	J	A	E	N	B	S	R
L	M	J	O	R	T	K	D	M	S	R	K	E	L	H	H	G
A	A	D	H	C	X	L	T	P	P	O	K	W	B	F	C	N
C	T	E	S	J	R	X	U	Z	O	D	O	D	E	D	G	E
E	M	T	X	F	H	J	M	B	L	B	D	S	Z	V	F	U

Vehicles 1 – motorbikes
Page 1

Lesson **2.2**

Motorcycles are here again

Jason: You've got a motorbike? Haven't you got enough money for a car?

Rick: It's not a question of money, it's a question of fun, and bikes are fun.

Jason: Your brother's got a Harley-Davidson, hasn't he?

Rick: Yes he has. Four stroke engine, three-fifty c.c., five speed transmission, it's a bloody marvellous machine.

Jason: You've got a Yamaha. I see. Has it got a four-stroke engine, too?

Rick: No, it's got a single-cylinder two-stroke engine, one twenty-three c.c.

Jason: Electric starter?

Rick: Oh, yes … here, it's quite easy: you turn on the fuel tap, turn the ignition key, put the gear level in neutral, pull back the choke lever, and touch the starter button …

Jason: The exhaust's a bit noisy.

Rick: That's right, but it's not a bad sound.

Jason: What's this right here?

Rick: A disc brake. There's a drum break at the rear. This here is a special exhaust system for more power.

Jason: You know that the Yamaha people want to build a motorbike with a rotary engine? It's in the paper.

Rick: Yes, I know. But I haven't got that much money. My Yamaha costs about six hundred and eighty dollars and I must say that's enough for a hobby.

1. Read the text and underline all parts of a motorbike mentioned.

2. Find the names of the parts of this motorbike.

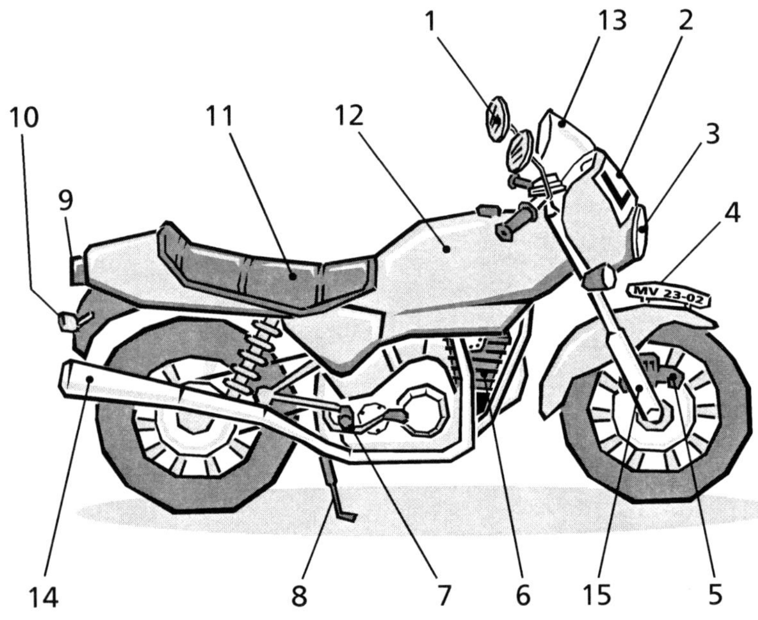

1. *side-mirror*
2. *L-plate (learners)*
3. *head light*
4. *number plate*
5. *brake*
6. *engine / motor*
7. *brake pedal*
8. *stand*
9. *rear light*
10. *indicator*
11. *saddle*
12. *tank*
13. *wind shield*
14. *exhaust*
15. *shock absorber*

other parts from the text:
four-stroke, fuel tap, ignition, gear lever, starter button, rotary engine

YES
I love it.
I agree.
I'm of the same opinion.
I think so, it's true.
Why not?
O.K.
Very good, let's go ahead.
That's my opinion, too.
Cool man.
Perfect.

NO
I don't like it.
It's absolutely impossible.
I simply hate it.
I don't agree.
I disagree.
I see things differently.
I don't see the point.
I don't think so.
I can't see that.
Rubbish! Oh, come on!
For God's sake, no!

Michael and his brother Steve don't have much money, but they both are motorbike fanatics. They are crazy for a Yamaha so one day they buy second hand. Still there are a few problems about several things.

1. Complete the dialogue by using expression of agreeing and disagreeing!

Jason: I *don't like* the look of our motorbike. Let's change the colour of the tank.

Rick: *I agree.* What colour are you thinking about?

Jason: My favourite colour is red.

Rick: How terrible. *I simply hate it.* Why don't we take black?

Jason: What a depressing colour! *That's absolutely impossible* How about blue?

Rick: Fine, *very good, but* I think the windscreen is too small.

Jason: *Rubbish, come on,* it's big enough.

Rick: *Oh, come on* I always get dust in my eyes.

Jason: *Very good then, let's* change it!

Rick: You know that we often drive long distances. Why don't we install a tv set?

Jason: You must be crazy. *For God's sake, no!* We are no millionaires.

2. Respond to the following suggestions.

People today earn much money.	*I disagree, on the contrary.*
Let's go to a cafe for some coffee.	*Very good, let's go ahead.*
When I'm 21 I'll get married.	*I don't think so.*
The running costs of a car are cheap.	*I don't agree.*
Most teachers are stupid.	*That's my opinion, too.*
The only understanding person in the world is my girl-friend.	*That's true.*

To be continued … more on page 47.

Vehicles 2 – cars
Page 1

Lesson **2.3**

1. Name the different parts of the car.

2. Which parts are in the electric system?	*Which parts are in the hydraulic system?*
head light	*brake system*
rear light	*tubing*
indicator	*brake fluid container*
battery	*shock absorber*
ignition	
starter, spark-plugs	

3. Frank is taking his first driving lesson.
Give him instructions what to do.

1. Open *the door*	6. Loosen *the hand brake.*
2. Sit *down* and fasten *the belt.*	7. Depress *the clutch.*
3. Check *seat position and mirror.*	8. Press *the accelerator.*
4. Take *the key* and start *the engine.*	9. Look *back* and *drive ahead.*
5. Press *the clutch* and shift *the gear stick.*	10. Put *the radio on.*

Vehicles 2 – cars
Page 2

Lesson **2.3**

4. Finding a fault in a car

If your car doesn't start in the morning, you should check three things first: the battery, the fuel level and the spark plugs. It is easy to repair these faults. If the battery is flat, you should recharge it. If it doesn't work, you should replace it. If the petrol tank is empty, fill it up. If the spark plugs are dirty, clean them, and if the gap in the spark plug is too narrow or too wide, adjust it to the correct width.

If your car still doesn't start, the petrol pump may be broken, or the fuel pipe may be blocked. If the pump is broken, it must be repaired or replaced. If the fuel pipe is blocked, take it off and unblock it.

If there is a loud CLICK! when you turn the key, the starter motor may be jammed. If it is, you can try to release it by pushing the car forwards and backwards in 2nd gear. If the car still doesn't start, the starter motor should be repaired or replaced.

Match the pictures with words from the passage.

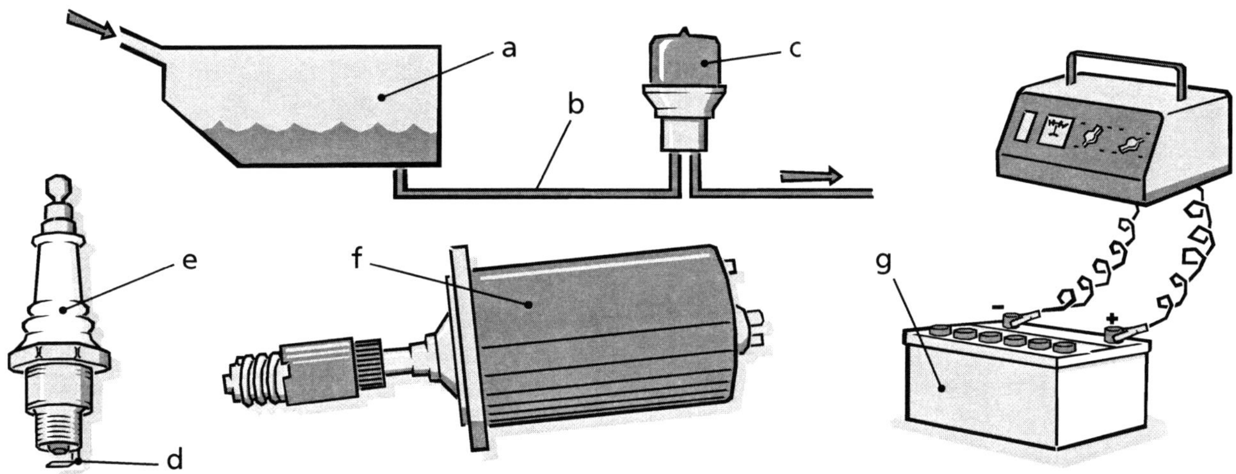

a) *tank* c) *petrol pump* e) *spark plug* g) *battery*

b) *fuel pipe* d) *the gap* f) *starter motor*

5. *Answer the questions.*

1. You check the battery. It's flat. You try to recharge it. It's still flat. What do you do next?

   The battery must be changed.

2. If the gap in the spark plug is too narrow, how do you adjust it? Do you widen it or make it narrower?

   You widen it.

3. How do you know that the starter motor might be jammed? What do you hear?

   You can hear a loud "click".

4. You push the car forwards and backwards, but the starter still doesn't work. What do you do now?

   The starter motor is broken.

Option 1
Vehicles/cars – How to check a spark plug

Lesson **2.3**

TODAY'S JOB

1. Remove the cover.
2. Place the spanner over the spark plug.
3. Rotate the plug anti-clockwise until it is loose.
4. Remove the plug from the socket.
5. Examine the gap and check that it is clean.
6. Insert the gauge in the gap.
7. Check that the gap is between 0.65 and 1.00 mm wide.
8. Replace the plug in the socket.
9. Rotate the plug clockwise until it is hand-tight.
10. Place the spanner over the plug and give a quarter turn clockwise.
11. **CAUTION: Do not overtighten the plug.**
12. Replace the cover.

1. What are these objects called?

a) sport plug ....

b) socket ....

c) cover ....

d) gauge ....

e) gap ....

f) spanner ....

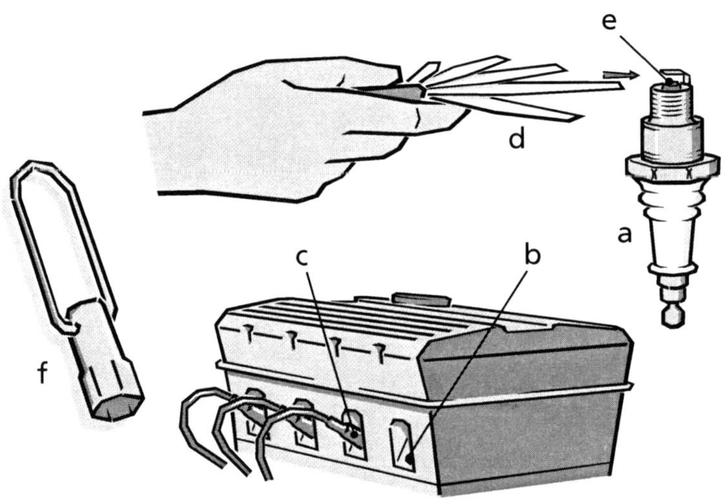

2. Are these instructions correct? Answer "Yes" or "No". Correct the wrong ones.

1. Turn the plug anti-clockwise, and ~~tighten~~ it. wrong: loosen
2. Look at the gap and check the width. right
3. Put the gauge into the gap and check the width. right
4. Tighten the plug with your hand. Then use the spanner. right

3. Which is the correct width of the gap?

0.5 mm (0.85 mm) 1.65 mm

4. What does a quarter turn mean?

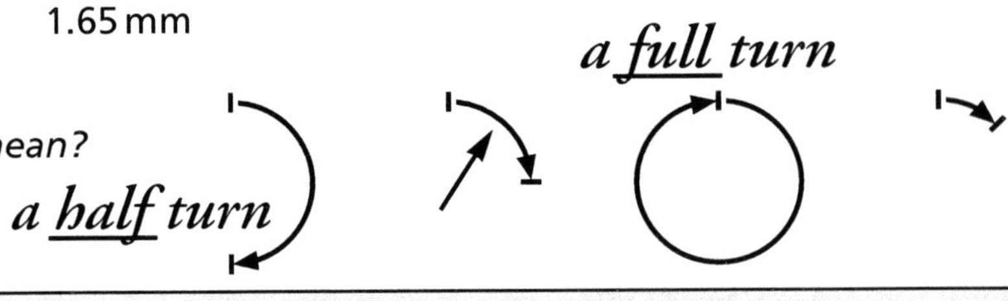

Option 2

Vehicles/cars – How to change a wheel

1. Read the instructions for changing a wheel and then put them in the right order.

1. Now unscrew the wheelnuts completely and remove the wheel from the vehicle.	*5*
2. Detach the hubcap if there is one.	*2*
3. Finally, check the air pressure and inflate/deflate the tyre to the recommended pressure.	*12*
4. Lower the car and with the wheel on the ground tighten the wheelnuts using the wheelbrace.	*10*
5. Apply the handbrake.	*6*
6. Jack up the vehicle.	*1*
7. Put on the new wheel.	*7*
8. Replace the hubcap.	*11*
9. Remove the jack.	*4*
10. Find the correct jacking point.	*9*
11. Replace the wheelnuts but only hand-tighten them.	*8*
12. Loosen the wheelnuts but do not unscrew them completely.	*3*

2. Name the components labelled in the diagramm.

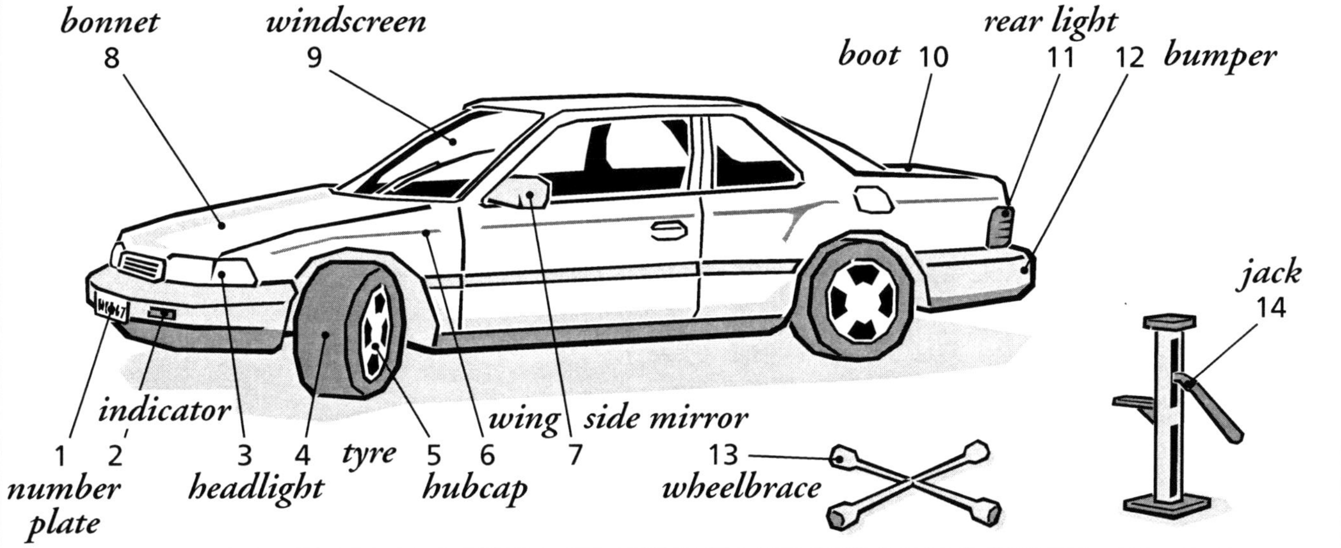

3. Explain briefly the function of the components labelled 2, 3, 6, 8, 10.

The indicators are for showing the direction you want to go.
The front lights are for showing you the way by night.
The wheelbrace is used for undoing the nuts of the wheel.
The jack is used for lifting the car up.

1. Form sentences this way.
This wire is malleable because it is made of copper.

1. *These goggles are brittle because they are made of glass.*
2. *This knife is very rigid because it is made of hard steel.*
3. *This screw is very hard because it is made of steel.*
4. *This cupboard is very light because it is made of plastic.*

2. Translate into English.

1. Gold ist schwerer als Eisen.
   Gold is heavier than iron.
2. Holz ist weicher als Metall.
   Wood is softer than metal.
3. Plastik ist biegsamer als Holz.
   Plastic is more ductile than wood.
4. Das härteste Metall ist Stahl.
   The hardest metal is steel.
5. Papier ist brennbarer als Plastik.
   Paper is more combustible than iron.
6. Aluminium ist haltbarer als Eisen.
   Aluminium is more durable than iron.
7. Heute ist wichtiger als gestern und morgen.
   Today is more important than yesterday or tomorrow.

3. ***Come on – off you go!***

					1	*F*	*U*	*E*	*L*			
			2	*M*	*I*	*R*	*R*	*O*	*R*			
					3	*E*	*N*	*G*	*I*	*N*	*E*	
		4	*S*	*T*	*A*	*N*	*D*					
	5	*I*	*N*	*D*	*I*	*C*	*A*	*T*	*O*	*R*		
		6	*L*	*I*	*G*	*H*	*T*					
	7	*W*	*H*	*E*	*E*	*L*						
8	*S*	*A*	*D*	*D*	*L*	*E*						
					9	*T*	*Y*	*R*	*E*			
					10	*T*	*A*	*N*	*K*			
					11	*E*	*X*	*H*	*A*	*U*	*S*	*T*
				12	*B*	*R*	*A*	*K*	*E*			

Brennstoff
Spiegel
Motor
Ständer
Blinker
Licht
Rad
Sattel
Reifen
Tank
Auspuff
Bremse

Solution: *FRENCH LETTER* ***???***

4. *Name as many parts as you know.*

see pages 40, 42, 45

5. *Respond by agreeing or disagreeing.*

Forms to be used from page 41 according to taste.

1. I hate Mondays. ....
2. Teachers earn too much money. ....
3. English lessons are the most outstanding events in my life. ....
4. A hamburger a day keeps the doctor away. ....
5. Smoking should become more expensive. ....
6. Never look a gift horse in the mouth. ....
7. Make hay while the sun shines. ....
8. Satisfying work is much more important than a lot of money. ....
9. If you really want something in life, you can get it. ....
10. The boss is always right. ....
11. Sex and drugs and rock'n roll is all I need. ....

Option 1
Parts of the body/clothes – and their technical meaning

Lesson **2.4**

1
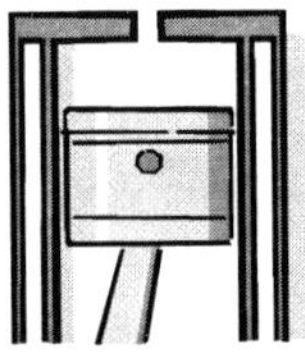
2
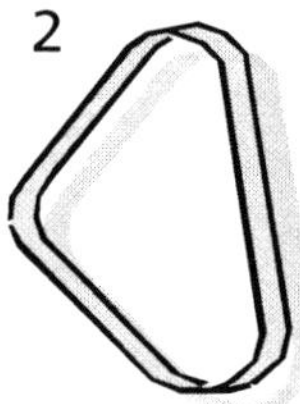
3

4

5

6
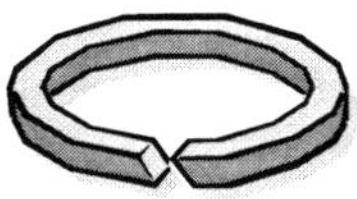
7

8
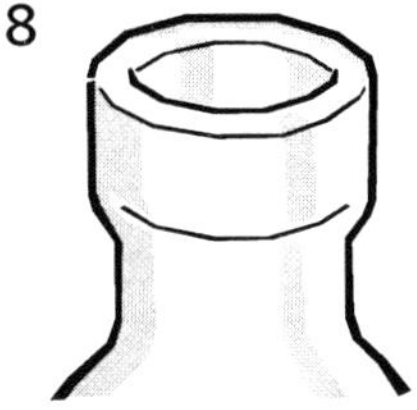

Technische Bezeichnung	English expression	Körperteil/ Kleidung
1. Ummantelung	*jacket*	*Jacke*
2. Keilriemen	*belt*	*Gürtel*
3. Verschlußkappe	*cap*	*Mütze*
4. Zahn	*tooth*	*Zahn*
5. Hammerkopf	*head*	*Kopf*
6. Spleißring	*ring*	*Ring*
7. Manschette	*sleeve*	*Ärmel*
8. Flaschenhals	*neck*	*Hals*
9. Bügel, Schwungarm	*arm*	*Arm*
10. Ziffernblatt	*face*	*Gesicht*
11. Zeiger	*hand*	*Hand*
12. Tischbein	*leg*	*Bein*
13. Nadelöhr	*eye*	*Auge*
14. Zangenbacken	*jaws*	*Kiefer*
15. Rand	*lips*	*Lippen*

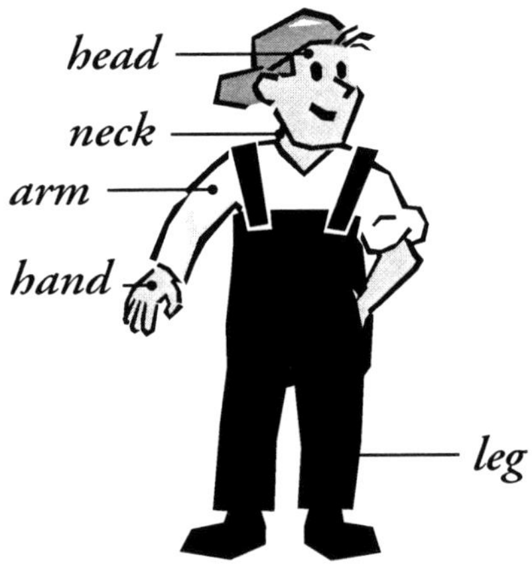

9

10

11

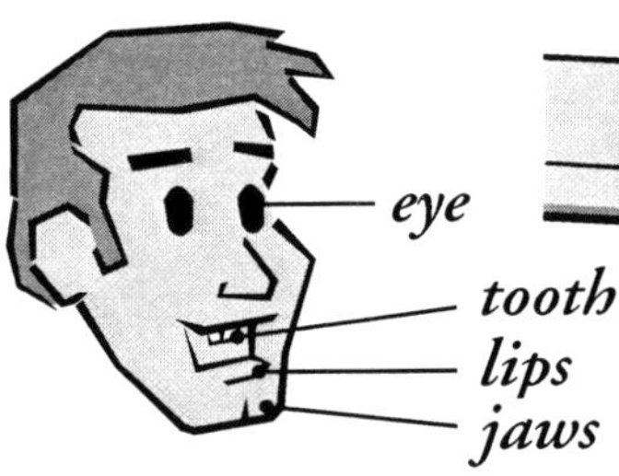

12
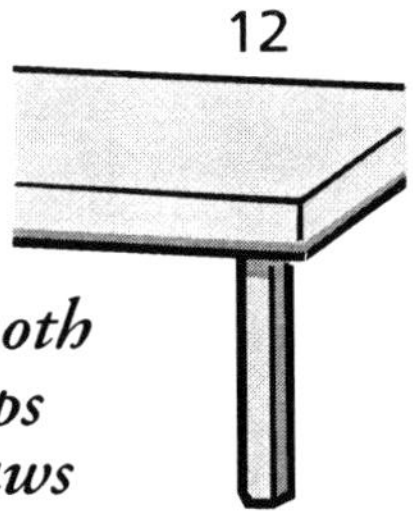
13

14
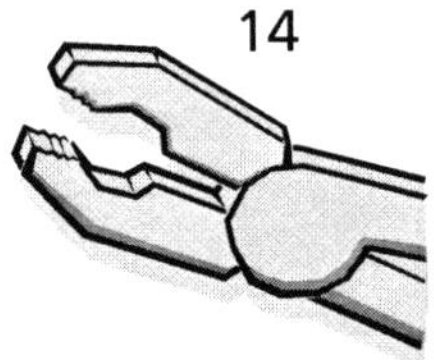
15
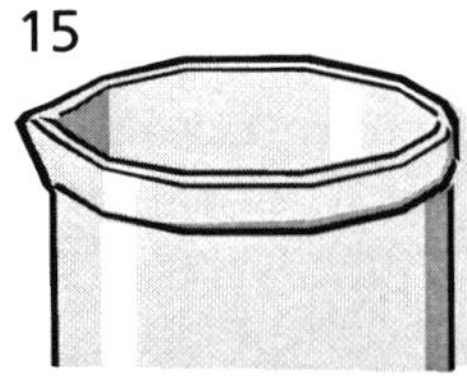

Option 2

Crossword – "Peanuts"

Lesson **2.4**

1 B	E	2 H	I	N	3 D		4 O	5 F	F
A		I			A			I	
R		6 S	O	U	N	D		7 N	O
	8 N				G			A	
9 W	I	N	10 D		E		11 O	L	D
	N		12 O	U	R			L	
13	T		N		14 O	B	15 E	Y	
	16 H	A	T		U		Y		17 A
18 I				19 U	S		20 E	A	R
21 N	E	X	T			22 I	S		E

CLUES

Across

1. Sam is ... the door.
4. The machine is on. Switch it ....
6. ... the alarm.
7. ... I can't.
9. ... the bandage round Sam's leg.
11. not new.
12. We are students. This is ... teacher.
13. Don't leave your saw on the floor. Put ... in the rack.
14. ... the safety rules.
16. 
19. We are students. Give ... our books.
20. 
21. First, then, ...
22. There ... a book on the table.

Down

1. A tool-...
2. This is Tom's car. It's ... car.
3. Not safe.
5. Next, After that, ...
8. 9th
10. ... touch it!
15. 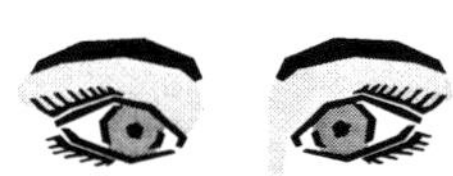
17. ... you a student?
18. ... the middle.

Option 3 – Page 1

GB – USA – Australia (Test)

Lesson **2.4**

Questions on GB

	YES		NO
1. Private schools take money from parents for the education.	X	1.	
2. Public schools in GB are private schools.		2.	X
3. Pubs in England close at 11 p.m.	X	3.	
4. Pupils at school have to wear uniforms.		4.	X
5. Cars in England drive on the left, in Ireland on the right.		5.	X
6. Cricket is a game which can last for more than a day.	X	6.	
7. Croquet is a game especially for women.		7.	X
8. Soccer in GB is played with an egg-shaped ball.		8.	X
9. Rugby is forbidden in Scotland.		9.	X
10. At Christmas everybody has a cheerful party.	X	10.	
11. The Republic of Ireland is an independent state.		11.	X
12. England consists of Wales, Scotland, and Northern Ireland.		12.	X
13. In Northern Ireland there is a conflict of Muslims and Christians.		13.	X
14. The IRA is a legal army to fight for the rights of the white people.		14.	X
15. Ireland is mainly Protestant.		15.	X
16. The population of Great Britain is about 60 million.	X	16.	
17. In GB you cannot buy alcohol on a Sunday morning.		17.	X
18. You must at least be 18 to get married.	X	18.	
19. In GB you don't have to do military service.	X	19.	
19. You mustn't drive a motorbike without wearing a helmet.	X	20.	

Questions about the United States of America

	YES		NO
21. New York is the biggest city.		21.	X (LA)
22. Most discos are only open for people over 21.	X	22.	
23. In schools you can also learn about cooking or car repairs.	X	23.	
24. In schools there are security guards.	X	24.	
25. Mexican people can work freely wherever they want.		25.	X
26. There are "Chinatowns" in LA and San Francisco.	X	26.	
27. If you have lost your job, there is plenty of support by the state.		27.	X
28. Insurance for health is not obligatory.	X	28.	
29. In the USA more than 25 % of the people are black.		29.	X (11%)
30. In California and Florida a lot of people also speak Spanish.	X	30.	

GB – USA – Australia (Test)

	YES		NO
31. The total of the population of the US is about 250 million.	X	31.	
32. Washington is the name of a city and of a state.	X	32.	
33. Many people never pay insurance for pensions or for their health.	X	33.	
34. "Shopping-bag ladies" go shopping every day.		34.	X
35. You can buy a gun when you are over 21.	X	35.	
36. The state fixes a minimum wage.	X	36.	
37. In most states you can only drink alcohol when you are over 21.	X	37.	
38. You are allowed to drive a car when you are 16.	X	38.	
39. There are no speed limits in the USA.		39.	X
40. Drugs are only a problem for black people.		40.	X

Questions on Australia

41. The total population of Australia is 16 million.	X	41.	
42. Aborigines are the original inhabitants of the continent.	X	42.	
43. Aborigines were not given full equality until 1967.	X	43.	
44. The country's symbols are emu and kangaroo.	X	44.	
45. The capital of Australia is Sydney. *(Canberra)*		45.	X
46. Australia is a very dry country with little rain.	X	46.	
47. Everybody celebrates Xmas at the beach because it is summer.	X	47.	
48. 80 % of the people live in only 5 % of the country. The rest is uninhabited.	X	48.	
49. Ayers Rock is a holy site of the Aborigines.	X	49.	
50. Emu and kangaroo are the only animals that cannot go backwards.	X	50.	

*1	1–	2+	2	2–	3+	3	3–	4+	4	4–	5+	5	5–	6	0
50,49	48,47	46-45	44-42	41-40	39-38	37-35	34-33	32-31	30-28	27-26	25-24	23-21	20-19	19-0	

Option 4 – page 1

Parts of the body

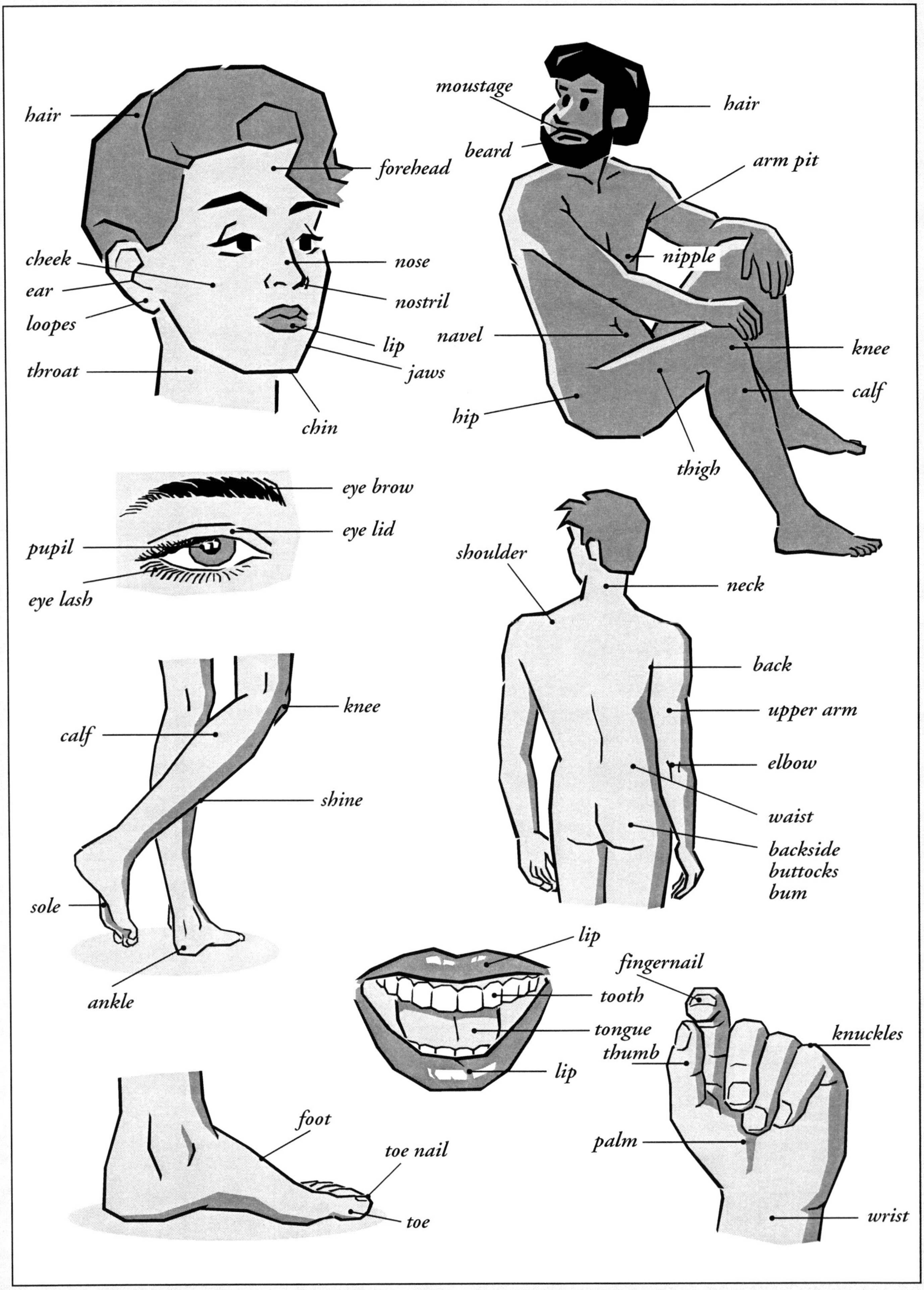

Parts of the body

1. *Show the parts of the body which are named by the teacher.*

2. *Complete the table underneath.*

head	trunk	limbs	organs	senses	naughty words
hair *eyes* *chin* *cheek* *mouth* *eyes* *forehead* ...	*breast* *neck* *belly* *stomach* *navel* *shoulder* ...	*arms* *legs* *hands* *feet* ...	*eyes* *ears* *heart* *liver* *kidney* *stomach* ...	*to see (eyes)* *to hear (ears)* *to taste (mouth)* *to smell (nose)* *to feel (skin)*	*?* *to be filled in according to taste*

3. *Answer the following questions.*
   1. What physical parts do you have a pair of? *eyes, ears, hands, feet*
   2. What organs do you have a pair of? *kidney, lungs*
   3. What are the five senses? *hear, smell, taste, see, feel*
   4. Which of the following words are used to describe what people look like? Use each item only once, then find two more adjectives.

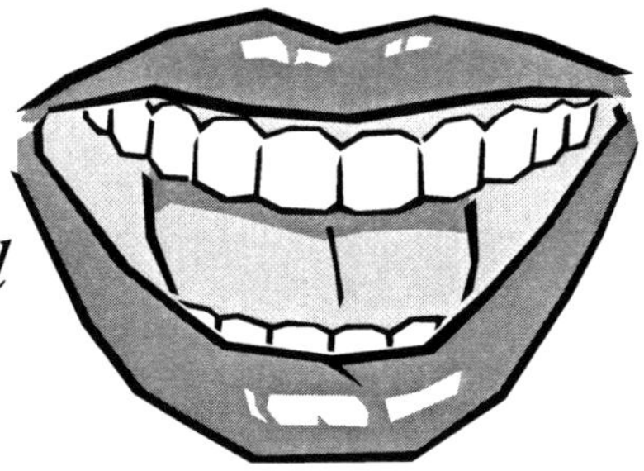

a) oval, round .... *face* → *ugly, square*

b) long, short .... *feet* → *sore, smelly*

c) thin, thick .... *legs* → *long, short*

d) fair, brown .... *hair* → *curly, fine*

e) ruddy, chubby .... *cheeks* → *cold, red*

f) large, big .... *nose* → *small, flashy*

g) broad, narrow .... *shoulders* → *small, thin*

h) straight, bent .... *back* → *short, hunchback*

i) long, flat .... *lips* → *red, big*

j) greasy, dry .... *skin* → *white, dark*

1. nose
2. face
3. feet
4. back
5. skin
6. legs
7. hair
8. shoulders
9. lips
10. cheeks

4. *Write a word snake with parts of the body. Ten words are minimum.*

Eyelbowristoe*aringfingersoeyelashheartoothand*

1 2 3 4 5 6 7 8 9 10

umbrella
hat
scarf
belt
boots
blouse
skirt
jumper
dress
shirt
jacket
pullover
tracksuit
pair of trousers
jeans
shoe
T-shirt
bra
petticoat
tie
vest
waistcoat
underpants
trainers
trousers
knickers
overcoat
socks
stocking

Clothes

1. *Name the types of clothes shown overleaf. Write down what you are wearing today.*

jeans, T-shirt, trainers, white socks, sweatshirt,
baseball cap, jacket

2. *Name 5 items for each section.*

underwear	leisure wear	formal clothes	working gear
knickers	*jeans*	*tie*	*boots*
underpants	*tracksuit*	*waistcoat*	*overall*
bra	*trainers*	*suit*	*helmet*
vest	*caps*	*trousers*	*goggles*
T-shirt	*sweatshirt*	*overcoat*	*gloves*

3. *Cross the odd one out.*
   1. blazer, anorak, ~~tie~~, coat
   2. ~~nightie~~, training suit, jogging pants, swimming trunks
   3. skirt, trousers, jeans, ~~leggings~~
   4. T-shirt, pullover, sweater, ~~tights~~
   5. body stocking, bra, knickers, ~~boxer shorts~~
   6. boots, slippers, sandals, ~~waistcoat~~
   7. *jeans*, *shorts*, ~~*glasses*~~, *underpants*
   8. *blouse*, ~~*socks*~~, *shirt*, *T-shirt*
   9. *stockings*, ~~*suit*~~, *skirt*, *scarf*

4. *Name five things you would wear at the following occasions:*

garden party, barbecue	*shorts, T-shirt, jumper, sandals, jacket*
wedding	*suit, shirt, tie, waistcoat, shoes*
interview for a new job	*shirt, tie, jacket, jeans, trainers*
theatre	*jeans, T-shirt, pullover, socks, cap*
holiday at the beach	*swimming trunks, shorts, sun glasses*
disco	*jeans, T-shirt, pullover, socks, shoes*
at work	*helmet, gloves, boots, overall*
in the gym	*shorts, vest, socks, trainers*
at school	*see disco*

OSZ Technisches Englisch lesson	**Test (A)** (30 words)	Datum: Klasse: Name:

1	1–	2+	2	2–	3+	3	3–	4+	4	4–	5+	5	5–	6	0
30	29	28	27,26	25	24	23,22	21	20	19,18	17	16	15,14	13	12	

OSZ Technisches Englisch lesson	**Test (B)** (30 words)	Datum: Klasse: Name:

1	1–	2+	2	2–	3+	3	3–	4+	4	4–	5+	5	5–	6	0
30	29	28	27,26	25	24	23,22	21	20	19,18	17	16	15,14	13	12	

OSZ Technisches Englisch lesson	**Vocab-test** (50 words)	Datum: Klasse: Name:

1	1–	2+	2	2–	3+	3	3–	4+	4	4–	5+	5	5–	6	0
50,49	48,47	46-45	44-42	41-40	39-38	37-35	34-33	32-31	30-28	27-26	25-24	23-21	20-19	19-0	

. . . . . . / 50 =

OSZ Technisches Englisch lesson 1.2.	**Test (A)** **Tools and jobs**	Datum: Klasse: Name:

Schraubendreher		Knopf	
Feile		to smooth	
Maurer		Schraube	
painter		Bolzen	
Säge		Klempner	
brush		foundation	
to pick up		Zirkel	
Zange		toolbox	
ausschalten		reparieren	
to hit		nut	
to press		lever	
ziehen		23	
to tighten		goggles	
nail		to bend a hook	
Holz		Arbeitsbank	

1	1–	2+	2	2–	3+	3	3–	4+	4	4–	5+	5	5–	6	0
30	29	28	27,26	25	24	23,22	21	20	19,18	17	16	15,14	13	12	

OSZ Technisches Englisch lesson 1.2.	**Test (B)** **Tools and jobs**	Datum: Klasse: Name:

light		carpenter	
Rohr		vice	
belt		bohren	
to empty		weich	
niederlegen		halten	
to pick up		wrench	
chisel		hacksaw	
schneiden		Kreuzschraubendreher	
Elektriker		Ringschlüssel	
to loosen		open spanner	
Glühbirne		callipers	
joiner		Hobel	
Rad		einfüllen	
Bohrmaschine		to plaster	
tailor		bauen	

1	1–	2+	2	2–	3+	3	3–	4+	4	4–	5+	5	5–	6	0
30	29	28	27,26	25	24	23,22	21	20	19,18	17	16	15,14	13	12	

OSZ Technisches Englisch lesson 1.5.	**Test (A)** **Prepositions**	Datum: Klasse: Name:

in the house		um den Baum herum	
under the table		in die Schule	
vor dem Geschäft		against the wall	
am Fenster		im Bett	
auf dem Tisch		durch den Wald	
behind the garden		up the hill	
outside the town		den Berg hinunter	
around the table		above the window	
between the girls		after the girls	
unter den Jungens		auf der Straße	
auf dem Schrank		at the butcher's	
out of the building		towards the factory	
along the street		where from	
über die Straße		zwischen den Bäumen	
off the tree		im Schubfach	

1	1–	2+	2	2–	3+	3	3–	4+	4	4–	5+	5	5–	6	0
30	29	28	27,26	25	24	23,22	21	20	19,18	17	16	15,14	13	12	

OSZ Technisches Englisch lesson 1.5.	**Test (B)** **Prepositions**	Datum: Klasse: Name:

im Haus		round the tree	
unter dem Tisch		into the school	
in front of		ins Haus	
im Regal		Baustelle	
Rad		in the cinema	
on the wardrobe		aufwachsen	
Leiter		to oversleep	
under the chair		über die Straße	
beside the table		Klassenraum	
below the window		to dress	
Steckdose		in diesem Moment	
Lineal		jeden Morgen	
Brett		Unterrichtsstunde	
pencil		cable scissors	
scissors		gegen die Wand	

1	1–	2+	2	2–	3+	3	3–	4+	4	4–	5+	5	5–	6	0
30	29	28	27,26	25	24	23,22	21	20	19,18	17	16	15,14	13	12	

OSZ Technisches Englisch lesson 2.1.	**Test (A)** **Properties**	Datum: .... Klasse: .... Name:

Complete the list, each item can only be used twice!!!

Nr	object	material	property	points
1.	box			
2.		wood		
3.			flexible	
4.		glass		
5.	window			
6.			combustible	
7.		rubber		
8.	hammer			
9.			rigid	
10.	scissors			
11.		cement		
12.		asbest		
13.				
14.				
15.				

1	1–	2+	2	2–	3+	3	3–	4+	4	4–	5+	5	5–	6	0
30	29	28	27,26	25	24	23,22	21	20	19,18	17	16	15,14	13	12	

OSZ Technisches Englisch lesson 2.1.	**Test (B)** **Properties**	Datum: .... Klasse: .... Name:

Complete the list, each item can only be used twice!!!

Nr	object	material	property	points
1.	hammer			
2.		cement		
3.			flammable	
4.		paper		
5.	knife			
6.			rigid	
7.		wood		
8.	goggles			
9.			flexible	
10.	cutter			
11.		steel		
12.		gold		
13.				
14.				
15.				

1	1–	2+	2	2–	3+	3	3–	4+	4	4–	5+	5	5–	6	0
30	29	28	27,26	25	24	23,22	21	20	19,18	17	16	15,14	13	12	

OSZ Technisches Englisch lesson 2.1.	**Vocab-test A** **Properties**	Datum: ... Klasse: ... Name:

Each term can only be used twice!!

concrete			
	steel		
		brittle	
screw			
	plastic		
		transparent	
scissors			
	nichrome		
		rigid	
goggles			
	cast iron		
		ductile	
plank			
	lead		
		expensive	
fire elements			
	brass		
		durable	
girders			
	tin		
		combustible	
springs			
	copper		
		flammable	
file			

1	1–	2+	2	2–	3+	3	3–	4+	4	4–	5+	5	5–	6	0
50,49	48,47	46-45	44-42	41-40	39-38	37-35	34-33	32-31	30-28	27-26	25-24	23-21	20-19	19-0	

....../ 50 =

OSZ Technisches Englisch lesson 2.1.	**Vocab-test B** **Properties**	Datum: ...... Klasse: ...... Name:

Each term can only be used twice!!

plug			
	cement		
		rigid	
pair of pliers			
	paper		
		combustible	
triangle			
	gravel		
		soft	
pipes			
	brass		
		brittle	
a sheet			
	copper		
		elastic	
wire			
	lead		
		malleable	
engine blocks			
	tin		
		durable	
electrical equipment			
	rubber		
		corrodable	
goggles			

1	1–	2+	2	2–	3+	3	3–	4+	4	4–	5+	5	5–	6	0
50,49	48,47	46-45	44-42	41-40	39-38	37-35	34-33	32-31	30-28	27-26	25-24	23-21	20-19	19-0	

. . . . . . / 50 =

OSZ Technisches Englisch lesson 2.1.	**Test (A)** **Properties**	Datum: Klasse: Name:

cast iron		ductility	
malleability		Druck	
elastic		Draht	
durable		Wasserleitung	
copper		wissen / kennen	
to retain		Dehnbarkeit	
rubber		nicht sehr	
springs		vergleichen	
properties		gebraucht werden	
water pipes		Stahlträger	
ductile		einfach	
to press		herstellen	
brittle		Elastizität	
teuer		to corrode	
Stahl		lead	

1	1–	2+	2	2–	3+	3	3–	4+	4	4–	5+	5	5–	6	0
30	29	28	27,26	25	24	23,22	21	20	19,18	17	16	15,14	13	12	

OSZ Technisches Englisch lesson 2.1.	**Test (B)** **Properties**	Datum: Klasse: Name:

behalten		to roll	
wichtig		equipment	
überhaupt nicht		tin	
ziehen		ductile	
Gußeisen		expensive	
haltbar		girders	
Federn		malleable	
Kupfer		to fracture	
Motorblock		brittle	
Keilriemen		lead	
Beispiel		mehr als	
Gummi		to remove	
weil		elasticity	
Stahl		battery casing	
zurückbekommen		brass	

1	1–	2+	2	2–	3+	3	3–	4+	4	4–	5+	5	5–	6	0
30	29	28	27,26	25	24	23,22	21	20	19,18	17	16	15,14	13	12	

OSZ Technisches Englisch lesson 2.3.	**Test (A)** **Motorbikes, cars**	Datum: Klasse: Name:

Fahrzeug		exhaust	
marvellous machine		spark plugs	
four-stroke engine		empty	
ignition key		width	
fuel tap		to unblock	
Windschutzscheibe		jam	
disc brake		to push	
Vorderreifen		forwards	
Stoßdämpfer		rückwärts	
bonnet		schmal	
steering wheel		to adjust	
Kupplung		to loosen	
wing		Auspuff	
tyre		to fasten	
Gaspedal		Anlasser	

1	1–	2+	2	2–	3+	3	3–	4+	4	4–	5+	5	5–	6	0
30	29	28	27,26	25	24	23,22	21	20	19,18	17	16	15,14	13	12	

OSZ Technisches Englisch lesson 2.3.	**Test (B)** **Motorbikes, cars**	Datum: Klasse: Name:

motor bike		blockieren	
Nummernschild		rear bumper	
back wheel		vehicle	
roof		Gebrauchtwagen	
speed transmission		to disagree	
Zweitaktmotor		wing mirror	
windscreen		Zündschlüssel	
choke lever		einstellen	
clutch		noisy	
compression		to depress	
spare wheel		exhaust pipe	
Scheibenwischer		headlight	
Wartung		accelerator	
rotary engine		kontrollieren	
fuel pipe		drum brake	

1	1–	2+	2	2–	3+	3	3–	4+	4	4–	5+	5	5–	6	0
30	29	28	27,26	25	24	23,22	21	20	19,18	17	16	15,14	13	12	

OSZ Technisches Englisch	**Klassenarbeit A** **Tools, jobs, instructions**	Datum: Klasse: Name:

1. Fill in the forms of to be.

.... / 3 points

John .... an electrician.

I .... 1,80 metres tall.

How many people .... in the workshop?

They .... all in the house.

The light .... on.

The bottles .... full.

2. Name these tools. What can you do with them? Who works with them?

.... / 15 points

tool	activity	job	picture
			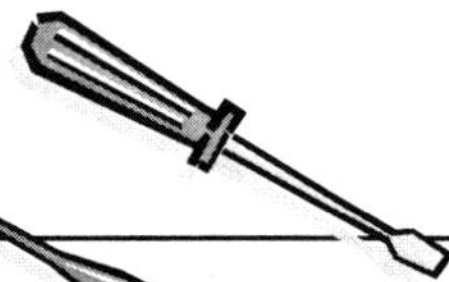

			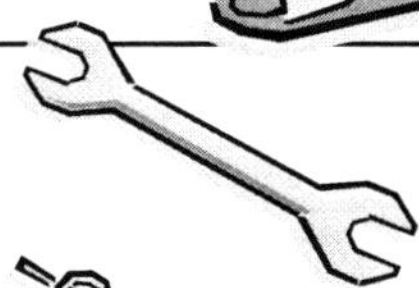
			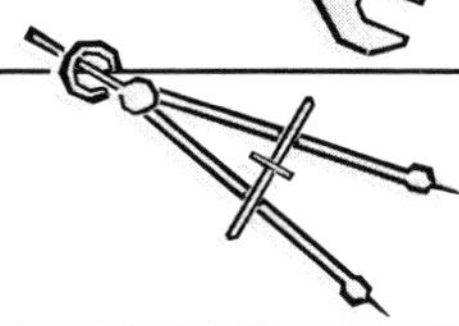

3. Fill in the missing words.

.... / 7 points

1. As a carpenter you often .... wood with a saw.
2. You can .... things with a micrometer.
3. A car mechanic .... cars.
4. With a file you can .... wood.
5. If you want to open a door you must .... the handle.
6. Before changing the drill you must .... the chuck.
7. At the end of the party you .... the light.

OSZ Technisches Englisch	**Klassenarbeit A** **Tools, jobs, instructions**	Datum: Klasse: Name:

4. Write these numbers in words.

.... / 10 points

3		61	
18		76	
37		82	
44		93	
59		25	

5. Right/Wrong?

.... / 5 points

	Yes	No
1. You make holes with a hammer.		
2. When I come home I open my front door turning the key clockwise.		
3. Before changing the wheel you loosen the nuts.		
4. When repairing the car you lift it upwards.		
5. When the film is over I turn on the video recorder.		

6. Give instructions.

.... / 10 points

1. The windows are open. 1. ....
2. Your English is bad. 2. ....
3. The screws of the wheel are undone. 3. ....
4. The light is on. 4. ....
5. The pipe is too long. 5. ....
6. The hammer is on the floor. 6. ....
7. I would like a bottle of beer. 7. ....
8. The fridge is empty. 8. ....
9. There are too many tools on this workbench. 9. ....
10. The party is over. 10. ....

1	1–	2+	2	2–	3+	3	3–	4+	4	4–	5+	5	5–	6	0
45	44,5	42,5	40,5	38,5	36	34	31	28	25,5	23	21	18,5	16	15,5-0	

...... / 45 points =

OSZ Technisches Englisch	**Klassenarbeit B** **Tools, jobs, instructions**	Datum: .... Klasse: .... Name:

1. Fill in the forms of to be.

.... / 3 points

Jack .... an engineer.

I .... 18 years old.

How old .... you.

We .... all students.

She .... very nice.

They all .... over 18.

2. Name these tools. What can you do with them? Who works with them?

.... / 15 points

tool	activity	job	picture
			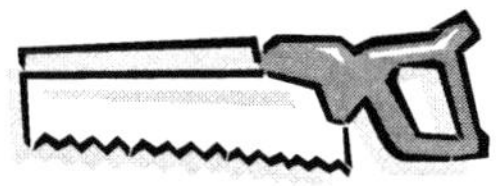
			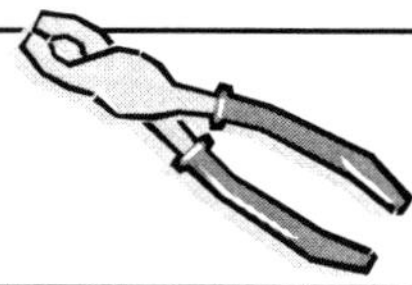

			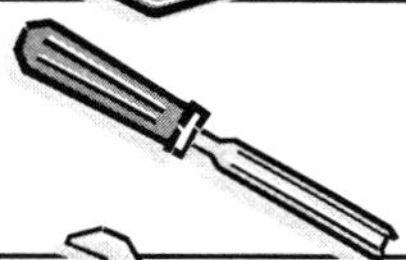

3. Fill in the missing words.

.... / 7 points

1. In the evenings you must .... the light.
2. When the ashtray is full, you must .... it.
3. The piece of wood is too rough, you can .... it with a file.
4. You can .... things with a pair of pliers.
5. To open a can of coke you .... the ring.
6. To watch tv you must .... the power switch.
7. As an electrician, you often .... wires.

OSZ Technisches Englisch	**Klassenarbeit B** **Tools, jobs, instructions**	Datum: Klasse: Name:

4. Write these numbers in words.

.... / 10 points

8		96	
13		81	
21		53	
64		62	
77		45	

5. Right/Wrong?

.... / 5 points

	Yes	No
1. In GB you first look to the left and then to the right when crossing the street.		
2. To start the car you turn the key clockwise.		
3. To close the toolbox you turn the key anti-clockwise.		
4. When repairing the car you lift it upwards.		
5. After repairing your car is put downwards.		

6. Give instructions.

.... / 10 points

1. The tank is empty. 1. ....
2. This piece of wood is too rough. 2. ....
3. The boxes are on the workbench. 3. ....
4. The screws are under the workbench. 4. ....
5. The door is open. 5. ....
6. Your walkman is on. 6. ....
7. The engine of your car is off. 7. ....
8. One nail is missing on this board. 8. ....
9. The nuts are undone. 9. ....
10. The lever is on the right. 10. ....

1	1–	2+	2	2–	3+	3	3–	4+	4	4–	5+	5	5–	6	0
45	44,5	42,5	40,5	38,5	36	34	31	28	25,5	23	21	18,5	16	15,5-0	

....../ 45 points =

OSZ Technisches Englisch	**Klassenarbeit A** **Prepositions, questions, comparisons, continuous form**	Datum: .... Klasse: .... Name:

1. Fill in the right prepositions.

.... / 5 points

2. Complete the sentences.

.... / 5 points

1. The saw is ....
2. The hammer ....
3. The spanner .... chisel and screwdriver.
4. There are .... the box.
5. .... these tools there is also a ....

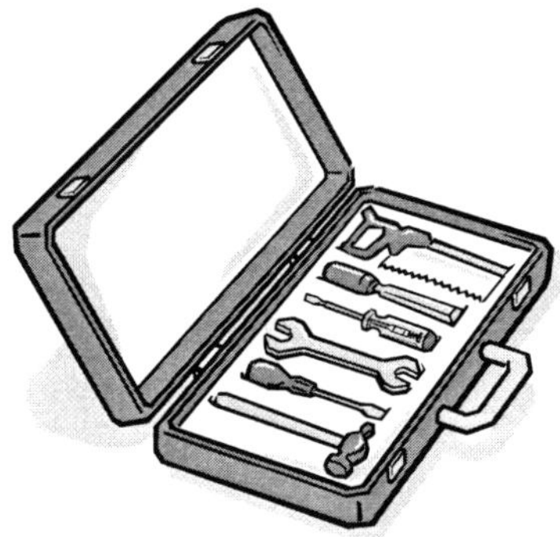

3. Form questions and give answers.

.... / 20 points

Where is the hammer?
It is on the wardrobe.

1. Where ....
2. Where ....
3. Where ....
4. What ....
5. What ....
6. What ....
7. What ....
8. How many ....
9. How many ....
10. How many ....

OSZ Technisches Englisch	**Klassenarbeit A** **Prepositions, questions, comparisons, continuous form**	Datum: .... Klasse: .... Name:

4. Fill in the right forms.

.... / 10 points

Today Rick (not, to work) .... he (to sit) in front of television and (to think) .... about his girl-friend. She is such a lovely person and he (to like) .... her very much. Sometimes she is very difficult and she (to want) .... things of Rick that he (not, to like ....). Something seems to be wrong today because she (not, to phone) .... at this moment. Rick (to wait) .... very impatiently (ungeduldig) at the same time. Now he (to dream) .... about a nice evening with her alone in the park. But then his dreams are suddenly over. His workmate (to be) .... at the door and says: "Come on, mate. Time for work."

5. Complete the table!

.... / 6 points

small		
		oldest
	bigger	
	more interesting	
		deepest
thick		

6. Right or wrong?

.... / 4 points

	Yes	No
1. David Copperfield is not the best magician in the world.		
2. Copper is more flexible than rubber.		
3. Rubber is the softest material.		
4. Wood is a hard material.		
5. Working is the biggest fun on earth.		
6. The Mount Everest is not the highest mountain in the world.		
7. The city of New York has more inhabitants than Los Angeles.		
8. A beetle is faster than a spider.		

1	1–	2+	2	2–	3+	3	3–	4+	4	4–	5+	5	5–	6	0
50,49	48,47	46-45	44-42	41-40	39-38	37-35	34-33	32-31	30-28	27-26	25-24	23-21	20-19	19-0	

OSZ Technisches Englisch	**Klassenarbeit B** **Prepositions, questions, comparisons, continuous form**	Datum: .... Klasse: .... Name:

1. Fill in the right prepositions.

.... / 5 points

2. Complete the sentences.

.... / 5 points

1. The window ....
2. The hammer ....
3. .... the table.
4. .... the box.
5. The table ....

3. Form questions and give answers.

.... / 20 points

Where is the hammer?
It is on the wardrobe.

1. Where ....
2. Where ....
3. Where ....
4. What ....
5. What ....
6. What ....
7. What ....
8. How many ....
9. How many ....
10. How many ....

OSZ Technisches Englisch	**Klassenarbeit B** **Prepositions, questions, comparisons, continuous form**	Datum: Klasse: Name:

4. Fill in the right forms.

. . . . / 10 points

Every working day John (to go) . . . . to his workshop at 6 o'clock. Today he (to arrive) . . . . at 7 o'clock because he had to go by bus. Normally John (to go) . . . . by car and every day he (to be) . . . . on time. Only today he (to be) . . . . so late. His boss is in the workshop, he is (to file) . . . . a big workpiece. His collegues (to have) . . . . a cup of coffee at the same time. They are very happy that John is now there. He (to say) . . . . "Hello" to them and (to walk) . . . . to his place. Now John (to prepare) . . . . his tools and workpieces, ready to start work, but at the same time the bell (to ring) . . . . !!! How lucky, it's lunch break.

5. Complete the table.

. . . . / 6 points

big		
		heaviest
	higher	
	more beautiful	
		widest
fast		

6. Right or wrong?

. . . . / 4 points

	Yes	No
1. David Copperfield is the best magician in the world.		
2. Copper is the softest metal.		
3. Rubber is the hardest material.		
4. Glas is a hard material.		
5. Working is the biggest fun of life.		
6. The Mount Everest is the highest mountain in the world.		
7. Route 66 is a very small road in Canada.		
8. A turtle is faster than a lion.		

1	1–	2+	2	2–	3+	3	3–	4+	4	4–	5+	5	5–	6	0
50,49	48,47	46-45	44-42	41-40	39-38	37-35	34-33	32-31	30-28	27-26	25-24	23-21	20-19	19-0	

OSZ Technisches Englisch	**Klassenarbeit** **Properties, cars, motorbikes**	Datum: .... Klasse: .... Name:

1. Form sentences this way.

.... / 5 points

1.1 The brush is made of wood and plastic.

1.2 The ....

1.3 ....

1.4 ....

1.5 ....

1.6 ....

2. What can you do with the above objects?

.... / 5 points

2.1 With a brush you can paint wood and metal.

2.2 ....

2.3 ....

2.4 ....

2.5 ....

2.6 ....

3. Write down the words for the indicated parts of this motorbike.

.... / 5 points

4. Agree and disagree. Use 10 different responses.

.... / 10 points

4.1 The Harley Davidson is the best motorcycle in the world. — 1. ....

4.2 Most people wear ugly clothes. — 2. ....

4.3 Smoking and drinking is very good for your health. — 3. ....

4.4 I would like to start my working day at 6 o'clock in the morning. — 4. ....

4.5 The optimal speed on motorways is 180 km/h. — 5. ....

4.6 Prince is the best pop-star of our times. — 6. ....

4.7 Teachers are mostly friendly persons. — 7. ....

4.8 My job is my life. — 8. ....

4.9 Girl-friends are very expensive. — 9. ....

4.10 Reading books is stupid. There are so many hot action films. — 10. ....

OSZ Technisches Englisch	**Klassenarbeit** **Properties, cars, motorbikes**	Datum: .... Klasse: .... Name:

5. You want to drive your car. Write down how you do it. What do you do first, second and then... . . . . / 10 points

5.1 . . . .

5.2 . . . .

5.3 . . . .

5.4 . . . .

5.5 . . . .

6. Your car is out of order. What can be fault? Form 5 sentences. . . . . / 5 points

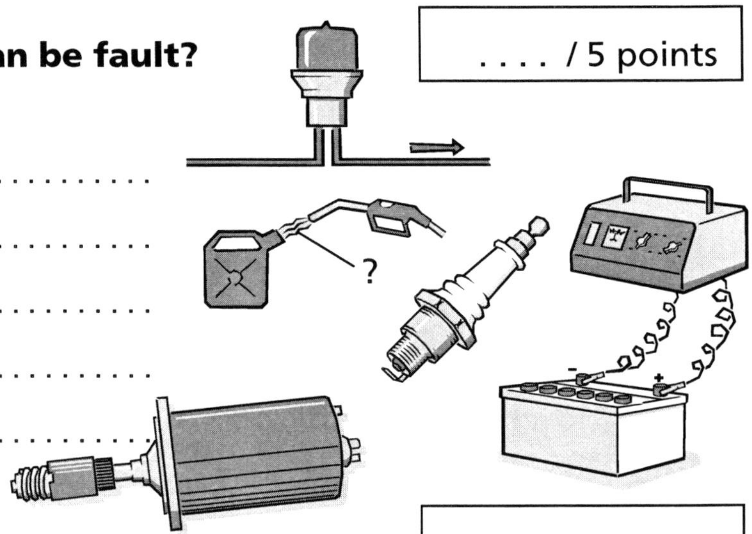

6.1 . . . .

6.2 . . . .

6.3 . . . .

6.4 . . . .

6.5 . . . .

7. Translate the following sentences. . . . . / 10 points

7.1 Beton ist härter als Plastik.

....

7.2 Plastikrohre sind biegsamer als Eisenrohre.

....

7.3 Holz ist ein weiches Material.

....

7.4 Glas ist brüchiger als Metall.

....

7.5 Benzin ist leicht brennbar.

....

1	1–	2+	2	2–	3+	3	3–	4+	4	4–	5+	5	5–	6	0
50,49	48,47	46-45	44-42	41-40	39-38	37-35	34-33	32-31	30-28	27-26	25-24	23-21	20-19	19-0	

OSZ Technisches Englisch	**Klassenarbeit A** **Cars, motorbikes**	Datum: Klasse: Name:

1. Write down as many words as you know. .... / 5 points

2. Give the German meaning for these objects. .... / 5 points

2.1 four stroke engine ....

2.2 drum brake at rear ....

2.3 five speed transmission ....

2.4 motorbike with rotary engine ....

2.5 special exhaust system ....

3. Write down the words for the indicated parts of this motorbike. .... / 5 points

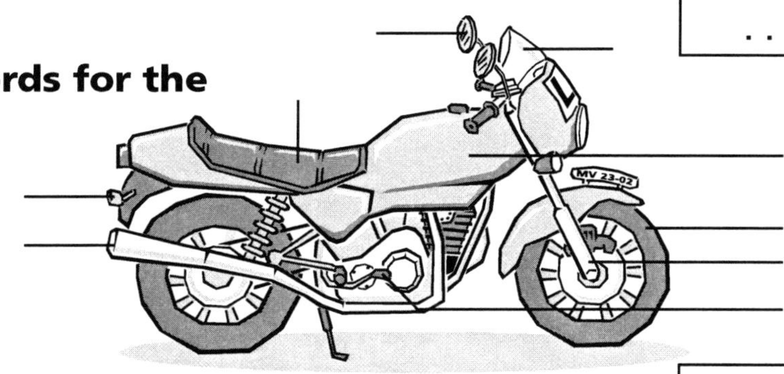

4. Agree and disagree. Use 10 different responses. .... / 10 points

4.1	The Harley Davidson is the best motorcycle in the world.	1. ....
4.2	Most people wear ugly clothes.	2. ....
4.3	Smoking and drinking is very good for your health.	3. ....
4.4	I would like to start my working day at 6 o'clock in the morning.	4. ....
4.5	The optimal speed on motorways is 180 km/h.	5. ....
4.6	Prince is the best pop-star of our times.	6. ....
4.7	Teachers are mostly friendly persons.	7. ....
4.8	My job is my life.	8. ....
4.9	Girl-friends are very expensive.	9. ....
4.10	Reading books is stupid. There are so many hot action films.	10. ....

OSZ Technisches Englisch	**Klassenarbeit A** **Cars, motorbikes**	Datum: .... Klasse: .... Name:

5. You want to drive your car. Write down how you do it. What do you do first, second and then... .... / 10 points

5.1 ....

5.2 ....

5.3 ....

5.4 ....

5.5 ....

5.6 ....

5.7 ....

5.8 ....

5.9 ....

5.10 ....

6. Your car is out of order. What can be fault? Form 5 sentences. .... / 5 points

6.1 ....

6.2 ....

6.3 ....

6.4 ....

6.5 ....

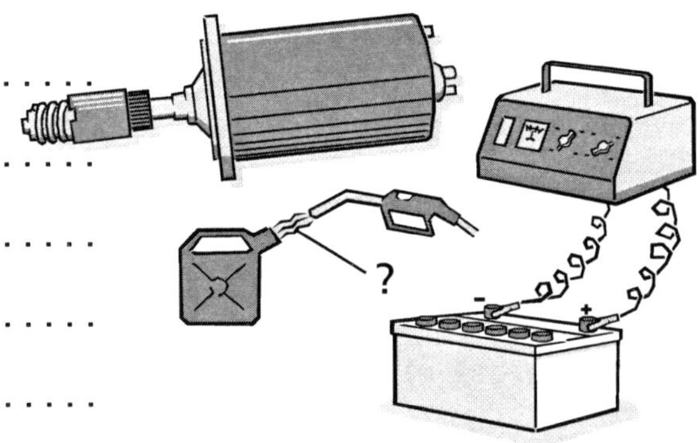

7. Translate the following sentences. .... / 10 points

7.1 Es ist leichter, kleine Fehler zu beheben.

....

7.2 Wenn die Batterie leer ist, muß man sie aufladen.

....

7.3 Der Wagen springt nicht an.

....

7.4 Du mußt die Zündkerzen erneuern.

....

7.5 Die Benzinleitung ist verstopft.

....

1	1–	2+	2	2–	3+	3	3–	4+	4	4–	5+	5	5–	6	0
50,49	48,47	46-45	44-42	41-40	39-38	37-35	34-33	32-31	30-28	27-26	25-24	23-21	20-19	19-0	

OSZ Technisches Englisch	**Klassenarbeit B** **Cars, motorbikes**	Datum: Klasse: Name:

1. Write down as many words as you know.

.... / 5 points

2. Give the German meaning for these objects!

.... / 5 points

2.1 two-stroke engine ....

2.2 noisy exhaust ....

2.3 closed fuel tap ....

2.4 drum brake at rear ....

2.5 single-cylinder motor ....

3. Write down the words for the indicated parts of this motorbike.

.... / 5 points

4. Agree and disagree. Use 10 different responses.

.... / 10 points

4.1	The Kawasaki is the most expensive motorbike in the world.	1.	....
4.2	Most people only eat junk-food.	2.	....
4.3	Drinking alcohol regulary is good for your body.	3.	....
4.4	I would like to win one million in the lottery.	4.	....
4.5	The optimal speed on motorways is 110 km/h.	5.	....
4.6	Prince is the worst pop-star of our times.	6.	....
4.7	Teachers are mostly stupid. Nobody likes them.	7.	....
4.8	My job is my life.	8.	....
4.9	Girl-friends are very expensive.	9.	....
4.10	The best films I have ever seen are from America.	10.	....

OSZ Technisches Englisch	**Klassenarbeit B** **Cars, motorbikes**	Datum: ...... Klasse: ...... Name:

5. You want to drive your car. Write down how you do it. What do you do first, second and then... .... / 10 points

5.1 ....   5.6 ....

5.2 ....   5.7 ....

5.3 ....   5.8 ....

5.4 ....   5.9 ....

5.5 ....   5.10 ....

6. Your car is out of order. What can be fault? Answer the questions. .... / 5 points

6.1 When must the battery be changed?   6.1 ....

6.2 When do you widen the gap in the spark plug?   6.2 ....

6.3 What happens when you hear a loud "click"?   6.3 ....

6.4 When the motor does not start, what can be the reason?   6.4 ....

6.5 What must be done if the fuel level is too low?   6.5 ....

7. Translate the following sentences. .... / 10 points

7.1 Der Auspuff ist sehr laut.

....

7.2 Wenn die Batterie leer ist, muß man sie aufladen.

....

7.3 Der Wagen hat einen starken Motor.

....

7.4 Du mußt die Batterie prüfen.

....

7.5 Die Scheibenbremse funktioniert gut.

....

1	1–	2+	2	2–	3+	3	3–	4+	4	4–	5+	5	5–	6	0
50,49	48,47	46-45	44-42	41-40	39-38	37-35	34-33	32-31	30-28	27-26	25-24	23-21	20-19	19-0	

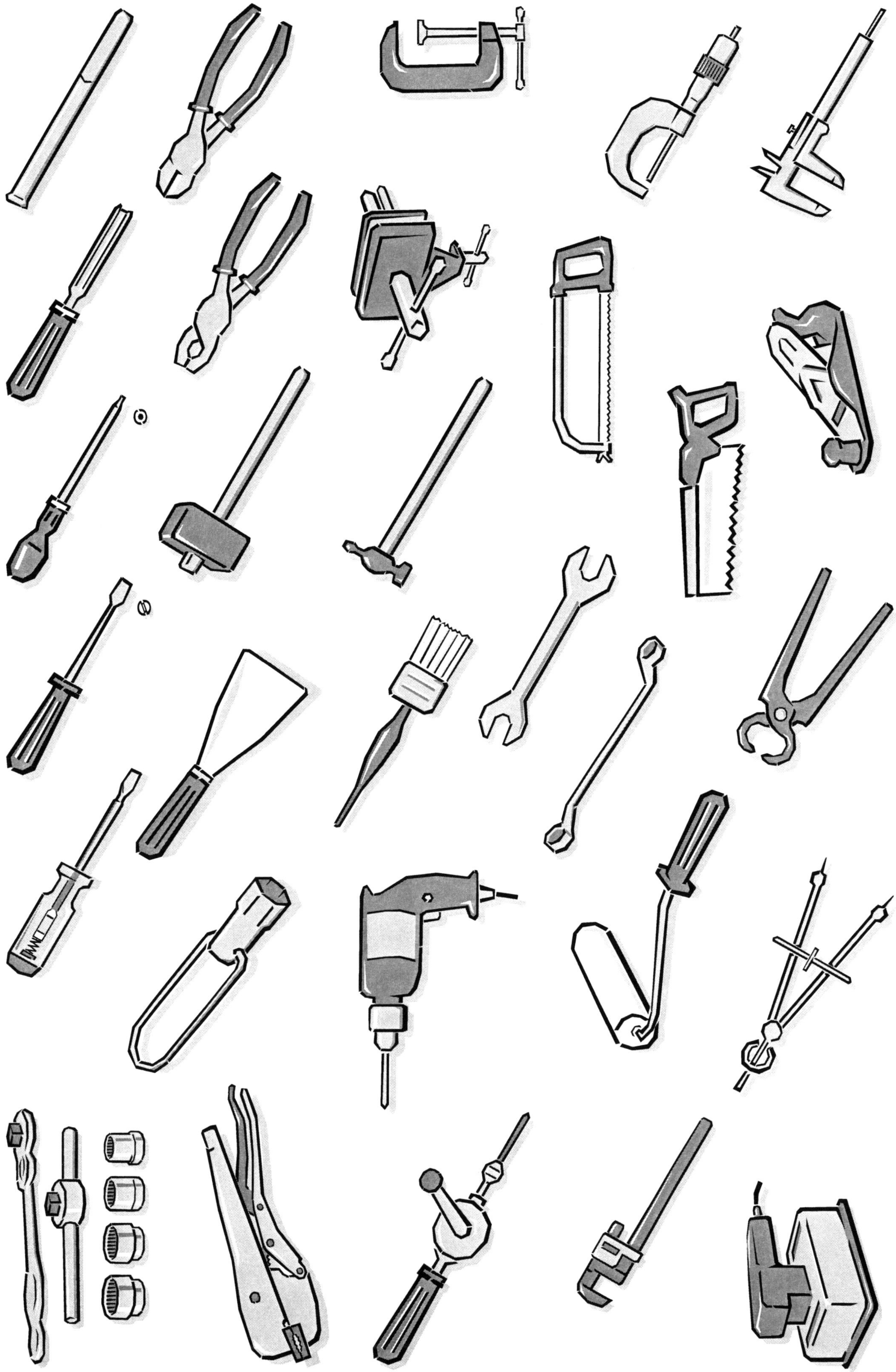

How many chisels, screwdrivers, mains-testers **?**

You have exactly one minute to count them all.

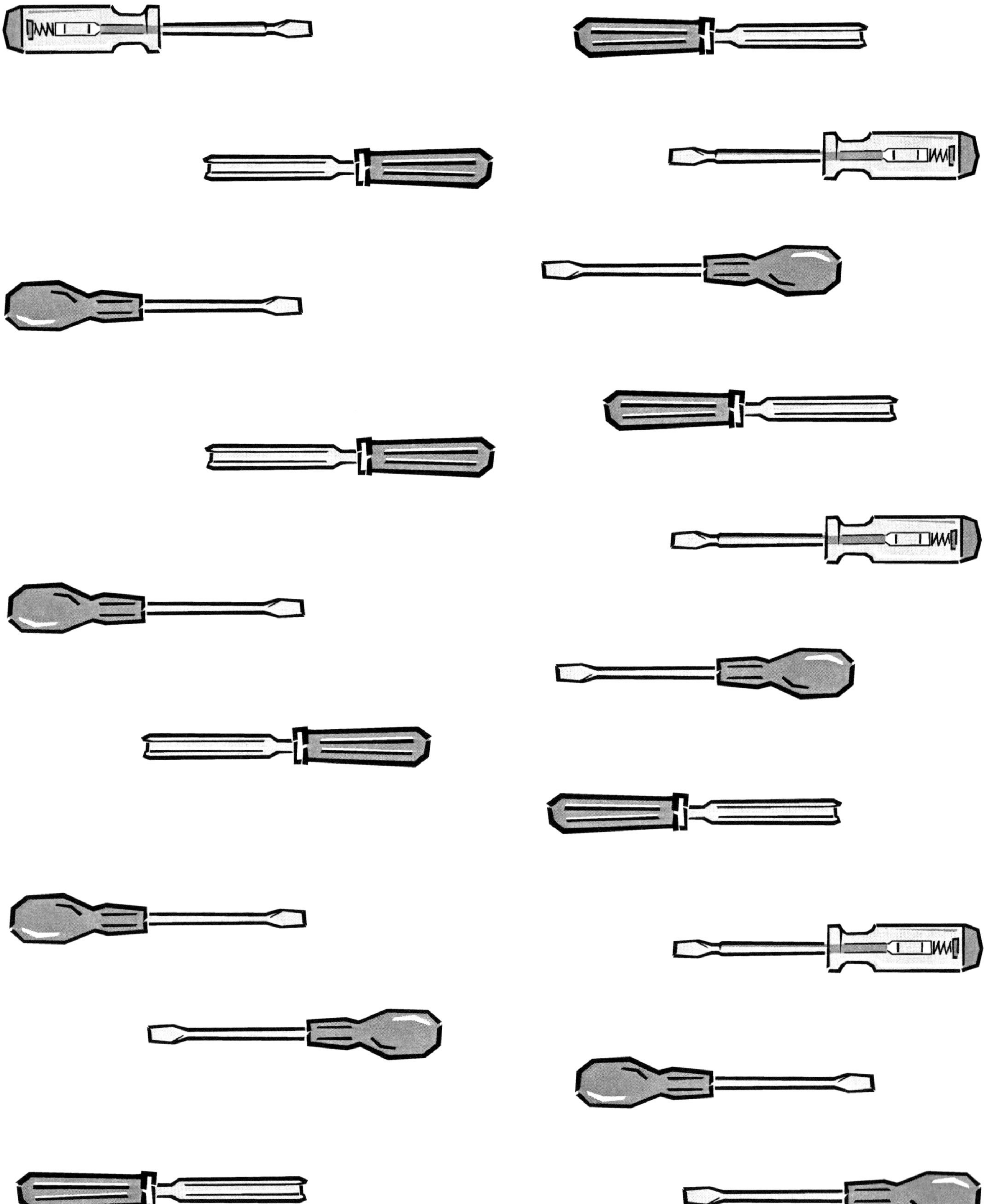

How many chisels, screwdrivers, mains-testers **?**

You have exactly one minute to count them all.

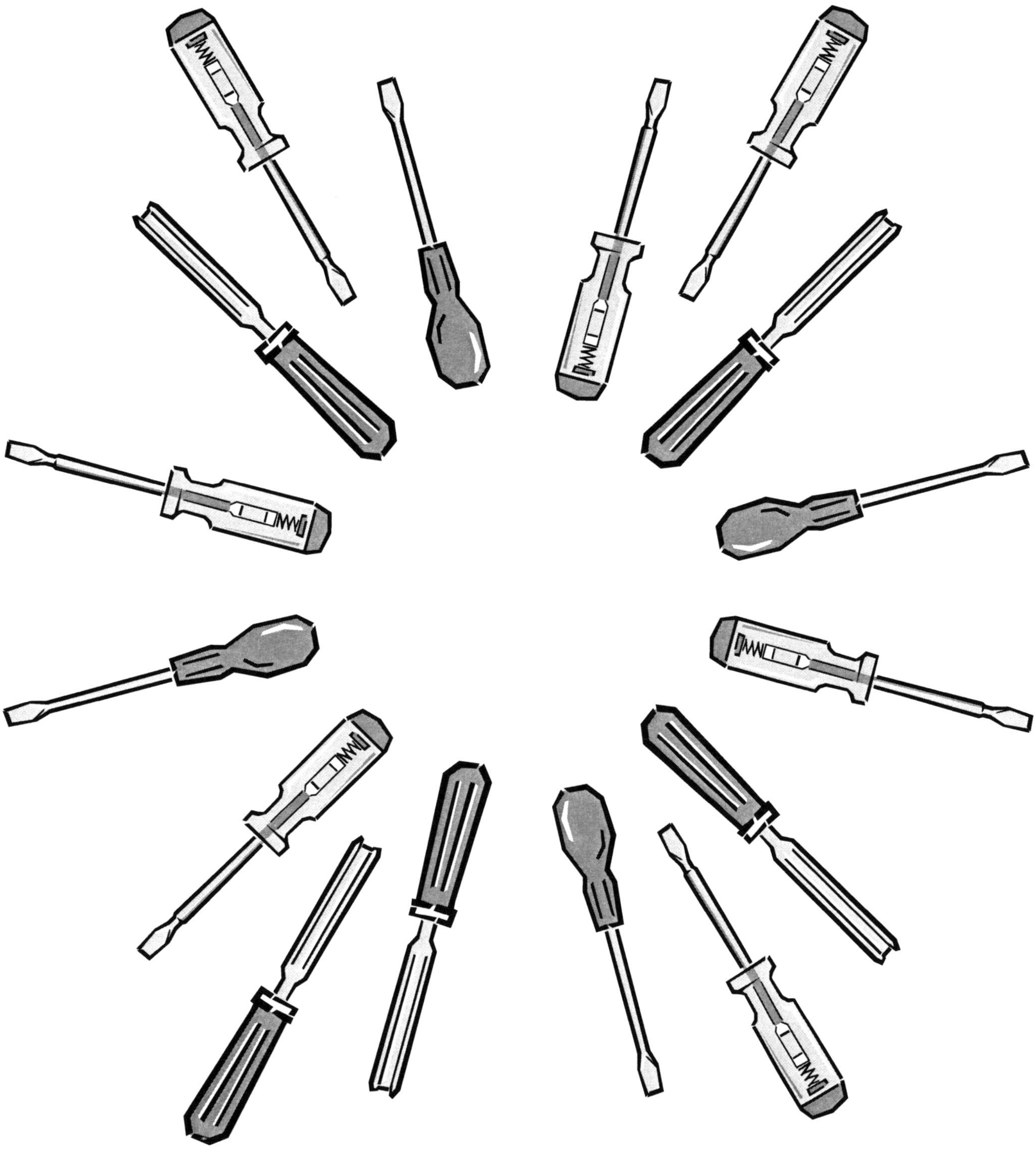

a)

b)

c)

d)

e)

f)

g)

OH-Folie "Workshop 1"

Where are the mice?

Use correct prepositions to say where they are. You'll have to find 15.

MV 23-02

OH-Folie "Car-interior"

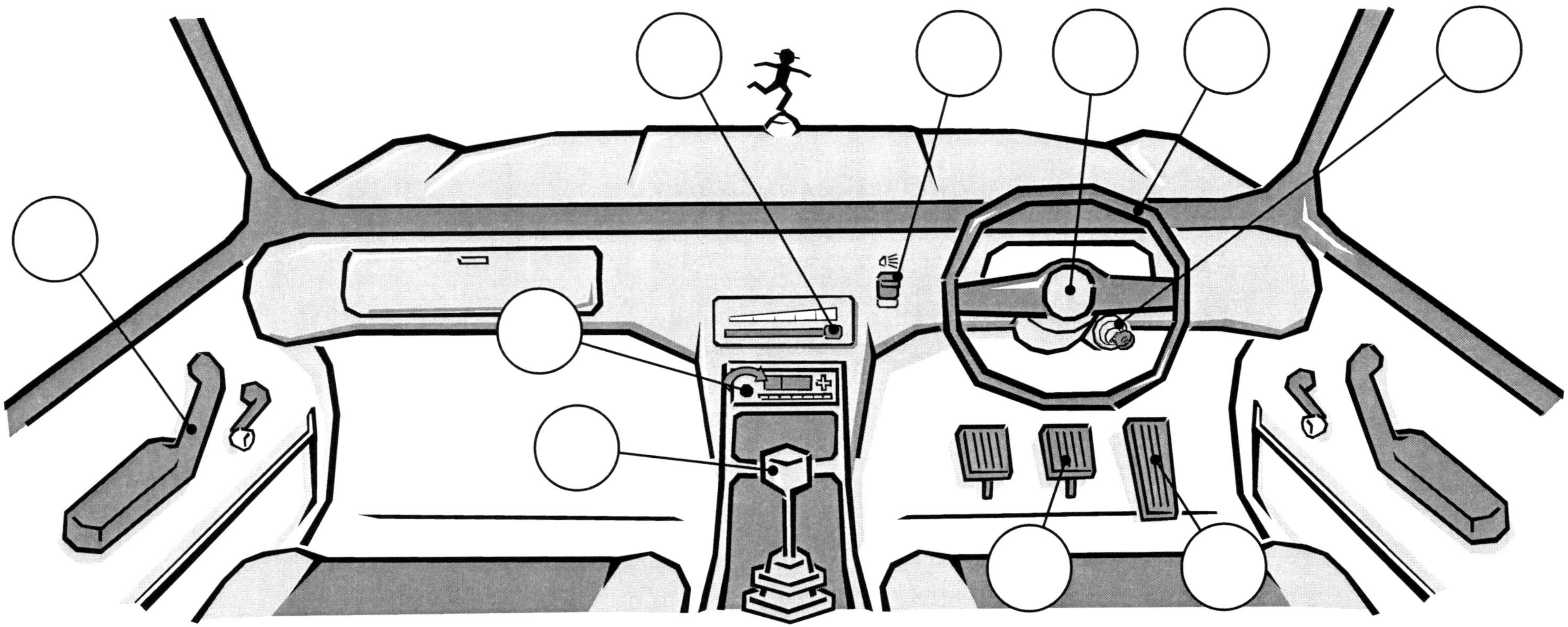

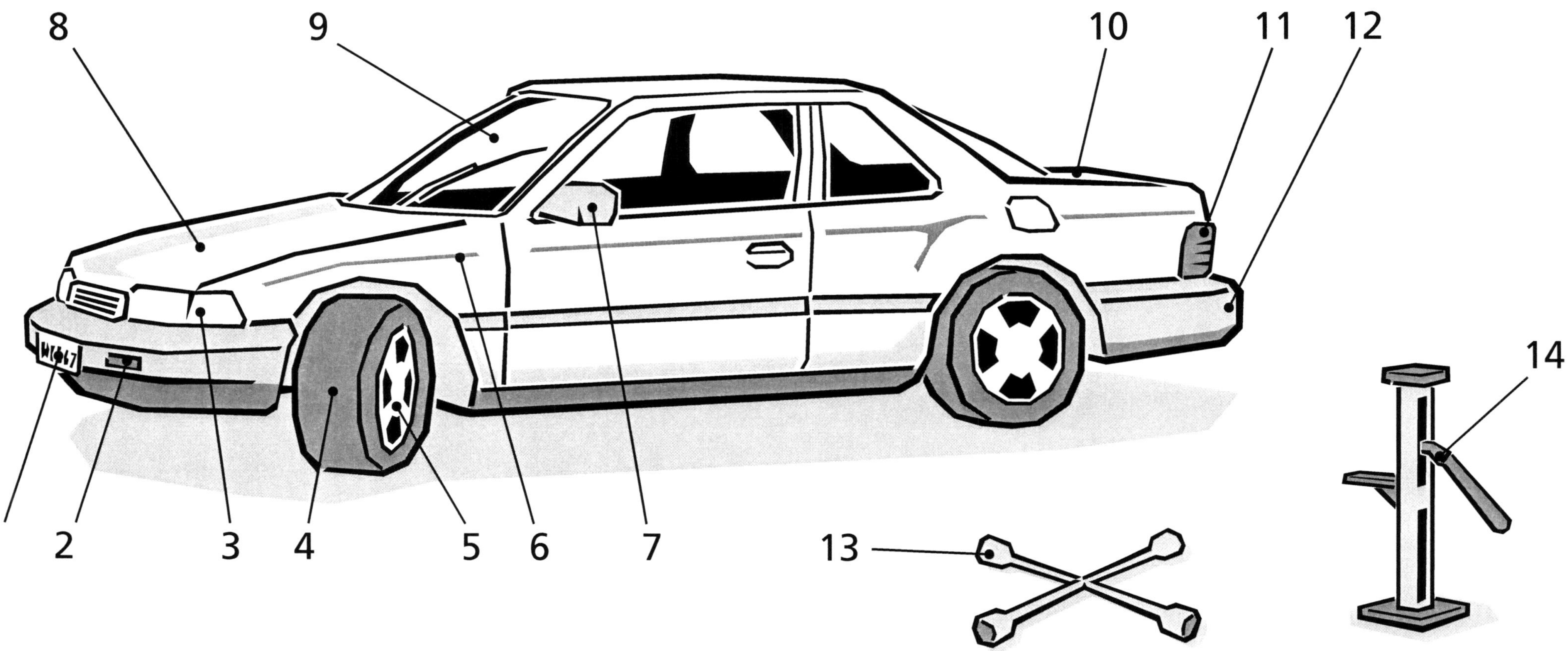
1
2
3
4
5
6
7
8
9
10
11
12
13
14

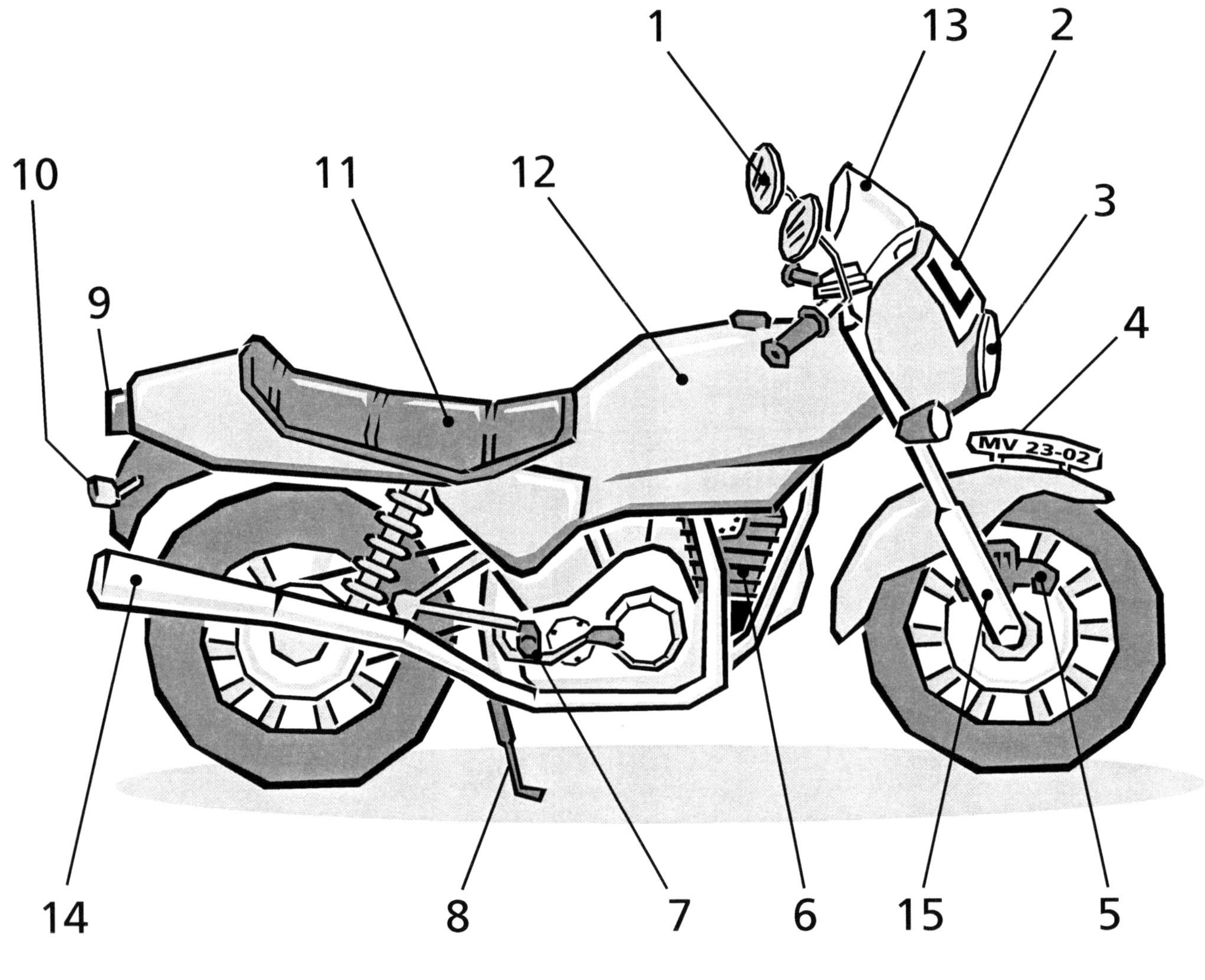

OH-Folie "Motorbike"

Quiz – questions on book 1	**Answers**
1. What is a clamp used for?	1. for holding things
2. Which tools does a metal worker use? Name three.	2. hammer, file, spanner, pliers
3. What is the voltage of a power circuit?	3. 380 V (Germany)
4. What can a mechanic do with pincers?	4. use for cutting wires, nails
5. What is the opposite of the word "empty"?	5. full
6. I would like to start an engine. What must I do?	6. turn the key clockwise
7. In what direction do you turn the screwdriver to tighten a screw?	7. clockwise
8. In which direction do you write in Latin?	8. from right to left
9. What is the plural form of "knife"? Spell it, please.	9. knives
10. Add 12 to 18 and multiply the answer by 5.	10. about 150
11. What do you do if you find 5 Deutschmarks on the street?	11. You pick it up!
12. What is the cheapest fuel for a car?	12. diesel
13. What do you need to smooth rough things?	13. a file
14. What do "AC" and "DC" stand for?	14. alternating/direct current
15. What are the colours for dangerous technical items?	15. red, yellow/black
16. What is the name of the fastest mouse of mexico?	16. Speedy Conzales
17. How many hours a day do children watch television?	17. 3 - 5 hours
18. What is heavier, one kilo of steel or one kilo of iron?	18. it is the same weight
19. Rubber is more flexible than copper, isn't it?	19. yes, it is
20. What is a plug made of?	20. plastic and iron
21. What sort of material is flexible?	21. rubber, plastic, copper, lead
22. Can you bend a concrete beam?	22. no, concrete is too hard and rigid
23. Can you burn a stone block easily?	23. no, you can't.
24. Why are pipes made of copper?	24. You can bend them easily.
25. What is wrong here? "A durable material corrodes fast".	25. wrong, cannot corrode
26. What are the most durable metals?	26. chromium, platinum
27. What is the most elastic material?	27. rubber
28. How can you store electricity?	28. battery
29. What sort of fuel does a motorbike take?	29. petrol
30. How many wheels has a car?	30. 6, 4 to run- 1 spare wheel 1 steering wheel
31. How many spark plugs does a diesel engine have?	31. none
32. How can you calculate the volume of a cube?	32. length to the power of 3
33. Multiply 4 by 10 and divide the answer by 2.	33. 20
34. Which tools does a joiner use?	34. mallet for woodwork
35. What do you have to do to stop a car?	35. push the brake
36. Another word for "to do up".	36. to tighten
37. Another word for "undo".	37. to loosen
38. What is the opposite of "to switch on"?	38. to switch off
39. Which profession uses a plane?	39. joiner
40. Which profession needs a soldering iron?	40. electrician

	1. What is a clamp used for?	2. Which tools does a metal worker use? Name three.
3. What is the voltage of a power circuit?	4. What can a mechanic do with pincers?	5. What is the opposite of the word "empty"?
6. I would like to start an engine. What must I do?	7. In what direction do you turn the screwdriver to tighten a screw?	8. In which direction do you write in Latin?
9. What is the plural form of "knife"? Spell it, please.	10. Add 12 to 18 and multiply the answer by 5.	11. What do you do if you find 10 Deutschmarks on the street?
12. What is the cheapest fuel for a car?	13. What do you need to smooth rough things?	14. What do "AC" and "DC" stand for?
15. What are the colours for dangerous technical items?	16. What is the name of the fastest mouse of mexico?	17. How many hours a day do children watch television?
18. What is heavier, one kilo of steel or one kilo of iron?	19. Rubber is more flexible than copper, isn't it?	20. What is a plug made of?
21. What sort of material is flexible?	22. Can you bend a concrete beam?	23. Can you burn a stone block easily?

24. Why are pipes made of copper?	25. What is wrong here? "A durable material corrodes fast".	26. What are the most durable metals?
27. What is the most elastic material?	28. How can you store electricity?	29. What sort of fuel does a motorbike take?
30. How many wheels has a car?	31. How many spark plugs does a diesel engine have?	32. How can you calculate the volume of a cube?
33. Multiply 4 by 10 and divide the answer by 2.	34. Which tools does a joiner use?	35. What do you have to do to stop a car?
36. Another word for "to do up".	37. Another word for "undo".	38. What is the opposite of "to switch on"?
39. Which profession uses a plane?	40. Which profession needs a soldering iron?	